HEARTFELT

THE DARK HOUSE COLLECTION

TWENTY ONE PIECES
BY **KIM HARGREAVES**

DESIGNS
KIM HARGREAVES

PHOTOGRAPHY
GRAHAM WATTS

STYLING
KIM HARGREAVES

HAIR & MAKE-UP
DIANA FISHER

MODEL
HANNAH WRIGHT

EDITOR
KATHLEEN HARGREAVES

EDITORIAL DESIGN
GRAHAM WATTS

LAYOUTS
ANGELA LIN

PATTERNS
KATHLEEN HARGREAVES, SUE WHITING & STELLA SMITH

© COPYRIGHT KIM HARGREAVES 2007

FIRST PUBLISHED IN 2007 BY KIM HARGREAVES, INTAKE COTTAGE, 26 UNDERBANK OLD ROAD, HOLMFIRTH, WEST YORKSHIRE, HD9 1EA, ENGLAND
REPRINTED IN 2008.

BRITISH LIBRARY CATALOGUING IN PUBLICATION DATA
A CATALOGUE RECORD FOR THIS BOOK IS AVAILABLE FROM THE BRITISH LIBRARY

ISBN-10: 1-906487-00-3
ISBN-13: 978-1-906487-00-3

CONTENTS

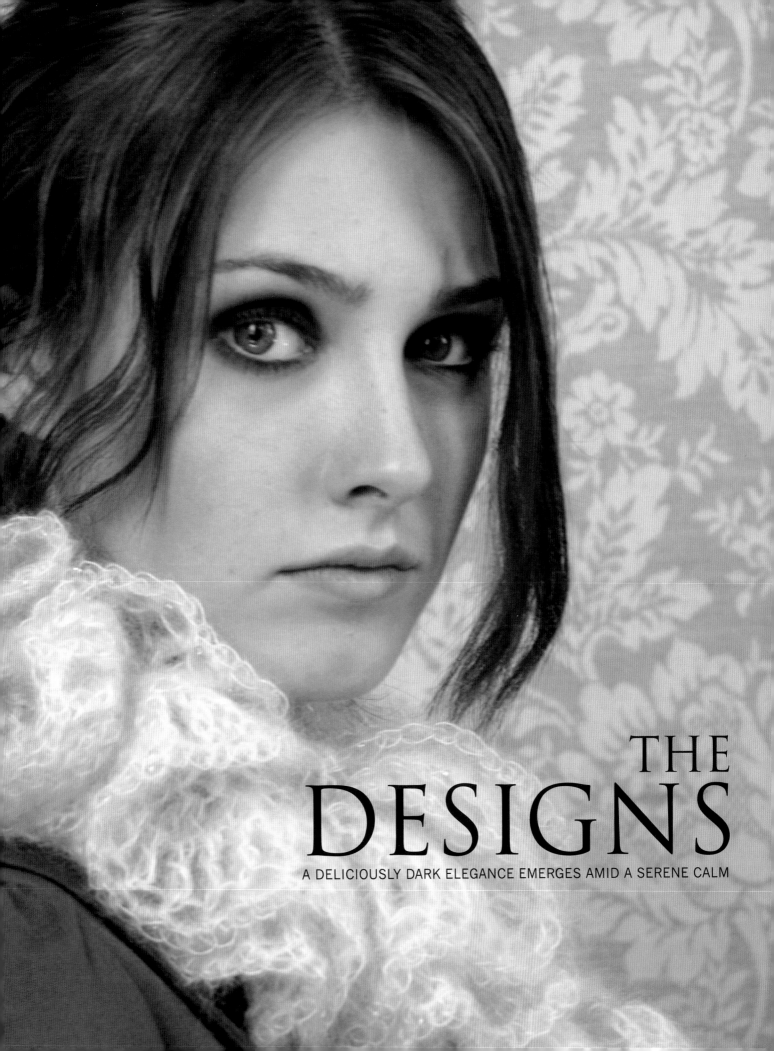

THE
DESIGNS

A DELICIOUSLY DARK ELEGANCE EMERGES AMID A SERENE CALM

AISLIN – A GRACEFUL SWEATER WITH FLOUNCE DETAILS, WORKED IN MOHAIR & SILK

GEM – A CHIC CROCHET BERET WITH BEADED TRIM

PRECIOUS – A BEAUTIFUL BEADED CARDIGAN WITH TIE DETAIL

CALM – A CLOSE FITTING SHEER SWEATER WITH EYELET DETAIL TO THE NECKLINE

DARCY – FITTED PEPLUM JACKET WITH A TOUCH OF THE EQUESTRIAN

WARD – SLEEVELESS CARDIGAN WITH DOUBLE BUTTON FASTENING

STORM – WORKED IN ONE PIECE, A SLEEVELESS TUNIC FEATURING ZIG-ZAG EYELETS

DUSK – AN UNSTRUCTURED TWEED CARDIGAN WITH OPTIONAL KNITTED BELT

ELIZABETH – A SOPHISTICATED JACKET WITH NOTCHED COLLAR & CURVED PEPLUM SHAPING

TESS – BOXY CARDIGAN WITH OPEN-WORK PATTERNING

EMILY – A SWEATER OF UNDERSTATED ELEGANCE, WITH SCOOPED NECKLINE & GATHERED SLEEVES

FLOURISH – FLOUNCY AND FROTHY, A CROCHET SCARF WITH BEADED DETAIL

AMORY – LACE PANELLING GIVES THE FINISHING TOUCH TO AN ELEGANT SWEATER

HAVEN – A COSY SCARF WORKED IN PANELS OF LACE

VALIANT – TEXTURED SWEATER WITH CABLE PATTERNING TO THE NECKLINE

FAITH – PRETTY BLOUSE WITH A GARTER STITCH PEPLUM & LACE PANELLING

NIGHTSHADE – AN ASYMETRIC PONCHO WITH A SLOUCHY NECKLINE & CORSAGE

ERIN – CABLE CARDIGAN WITH SLIGHT A-LINE SHAPING & CONTRASTING BUTTON DETAIL

CHERISH – FITTED SHRUG WITH SLIGHTLY FLARED SLEEVES & SINGLE BUTTON FASTENING

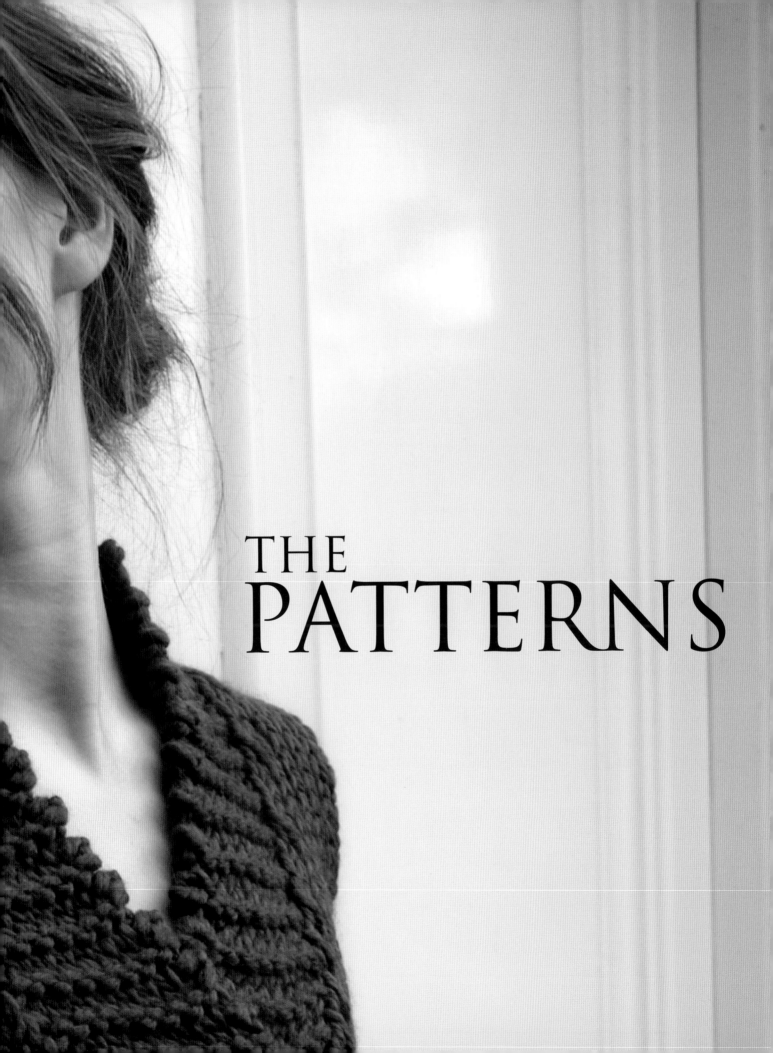

THE
PATTERNS

AISLIN

GRACEFUL SWEATER WITH FLOUNCE DETAILS

Recommendation

Suitable for the knitter with a little experience.
Please see pages 8 & 9 for photographs.

	XS	S	M	L	XL	XXL	
To fit	**81**	**86**	**91**	**97**	**102**	**109**	cm
bust	32	34	36	38	40	43	in

Rowan Kidsilk Aura

| 7 | 8 | 9 | 9 | 10 | 10 x 25gm |

Needles

1 pair 4 ½ mm (no 7) (US 7) needles
1 pair 5 mm (no 6) (US 8) needles
1 pair 5 ½ mm (no 5) (US 9) needles

Tension

15 sts and 20 rows to 10cm measured over
stocking stitch using 5 ½ mm (US 9) needles

BACK

Cast on 238 (246: 274: 282: 310: 322) sts using
5 ½ mm (US 9) needles and work flounce as
folls:
Row 1 (RS) (dec): (Sl 1, K1, psso) to end.
119 (123: 137: 141: 155: 161) sts.
Row 2: P3 (5: 3: 5: 3: 6), (K5, P4) 12 (12:
14: 14: 16: 16) times, K5, P3 (5: 3: 5: 3: 6).
Row 3: K3 (5: 3: 5: 3: 6), (P5, K4) 12 (12:
14: 14: 16: 16) times, P5, K3 (5: 3: 5: 3: 6).
Work 3 (3: 3: 5: 5: 5) rows on sts as set,
ending with a WS row.
Next row (RS)(dec): K3 (5: 3: 5: 3: 6),
(P1, P3tog, P1, K4) 12 (12: 14: 14: 16: 16)
times, P1, P3tog, P1, K3 (5: 3: 5: 3: 6).
93 (97: 107: 111: 121: 127) sts.
Next row: P3 (5: 3: 5: 3: 6), (K3, P4) 12 (12:
14: 14: 16: 16) times, K3, P3 (5: 3: 5: 3: 6).
Work 4 rows on sts as set, end with a WS row.
Next row (RS)(dec): K3 (5: 3: 5: 3: 6), (P3tog,
K4) 12 (12: 14: 14: 16: 16) times, P3tog, K3
(5: 3: 5: 3: 6). 67 (71: 77: 81: 87: 93) sts.
Next row: P3 (5: 3: 5: 3: 6), (K1, P4) 12 (12:
14: 14: 16: 16) times, K1, P3 (5: 3: 5: 3: 6.
Work 4 rows on sts as set, end with a WS row.
Next row (RS)(dec): K0 (2: 0: 2: 0: 3), (K3,
K2tog) 13 (13: 15: 15: 17: 17) times, K2 (4:
2: 4: 2: 5). 54 (58: 62: 66: 70: 76) sts.
Purl 1 row.
Cont in st st shaping sides as folls:
Work 2 rows.
Next row (RS) (dec): K2, K2tog, K to last 4
sts, K2tog tbl, K2. 52 (56: 60: 64: 68: 74) sts.
Work 5 rows.
Dec 1 st as before at each end of next row.
50 (54: 58: 62: 66: 72) sts.
Work 15 rows, ending with a WS row.
Next row (RS)(inc): K2, M1, K to last 2 sts,
M1, K2. 52 (56: 60: 64: 68: 74) sts.
Work 7 rows, ending with a WS row.
Inc 1 st as before at each end of next row and
3 foll 6th rows.
60 (64: 68: 72: 76: 82) sts.
Work straight until back measures 39 (39: 40:
40: 40: 40)cm from cast on edge, ending with
a WS row.

Shape armholes

Cast off 3 sts at beg of next 2 rows.
54 (58: 62: 66: 70: 76) sts.
Dec 1 st at each end of next 3 (3: 3: 5: 5: 5)
rows, then on 1 (2: 2: 1: 2: 3) foll alt rows,
and then on foll 4th row.
44 (46: 50: 52: 54: 58) sts. **
Work straight until armhole measures 11 (12:
12: 13: 13: 13)cm, ending with a WS row.
Work 10 (10: 10: 12: 10: 8) rows, ending with
a WS row.

Shape back neck

Next row (RS): K11 (12: 12: 12: 12: 12)
and turn, leaving rem sts on a holder.
Work each side of neck separately.
Cast off 3 sts, work to end.
8 (9: 9: 9: 9: 9) sts.
Dec 1 st at neck edge on next 5 rows and then
on 1 (2: 2: 2: 2: 2) foll alt rows. 2 sts.
Work 5 (3: 3: 3: 5: 7) rows, ending with a
WS row.
Cast off.
With RS facing rejoin yarn to rem sts, cast off
centre 22 (22: 26: 28: 30: 34) sts, K to end.
Complete to match first side, reversing
shaping.

FRONT

Work as given for back to **.
Work straight until front is 6 rows shorter
than back to beg of neck shaping, ending
with a WS row.
Next row (RS): K11 (12: 12: 12: 12: 12)
and turn, leaving rem sts on a holder.
Work each side of neck separately.
Cast off 3 sts, work to end.
8 (9: 9: 9: 9: 9) sts.
Dec 1 st at neck edge on next 3 rows, then on
2 (3: 3: 3: 3: 3) foll alt rows, and then on foll
4th row. 2 sts.
Work 7 (5: 5: 5: 7: 9) rows, ending with a WS row.
Cast off.
With RS facing rejoin yarn to rem sts, cast off
centre 22 (22: 26: 28: 30: 34) sts, K to end.
Complete to match first side, reversing
shaping.

SLEEVES (both alike)

Cast on 130 (134: 138: 142: 166: 170) sts using 5 ½ mm (US 9) needles and work lower edge and set stitches for flounce as folls:

Row 1 (RS) (dec): (Sl 1, K1, psso) to end. 65 (67: 69: 71: 83: 85) sts.

Row 2: P3 (4: 5: 6: 3: 4), (K5, P4) 6 (6: 6: 6: 8: 8) times, K5, P3 (4: 5: 6: 3: 4).

Row 3: K3 (4: 5: 6: 3: 4), (P5, K4) 6 (6: 6: 6: 8: 8) times, P5, K3 (4: 5: 6: 3: 4).

Work 3 rows on sts as set, end with a WS row.

Row 7 (RS) (dec): K3 (4: 5: 6: 3: 4), (P1, P3tog, P1, K4) 6 (6: 6: 6: 8: 8) times, P1, P3tog, P1, K3 (4: 5: 6: 3: 4). 51 (53: 55: 57: 65: 67) sts.

Work 5 rows on sts as set, end with a WS row.

Row 13 (RS) (dec): K3 (4: 5: 6: 3: 4), (P3tog, K4) 6 (6: 6: 6: 8: 8) times, P3tog, K3 (4: 5: 6: 3: 4). 37 (39: 41: 43: 47: 49) sts.

Work 5 rows on sts as set.

Row 19 (RS) (dec): K0 (1: 2: 3: 0: 1), (K3, K2tog) 7 (7: 7: 7: 9: 9) times, K2 (3: 4: 5: 2: 3). 30 (32: 34: 36: 38: 40) sts.

Next row (WS): Purl.

Cont in st st shaping sides as folls:

Next row (RS)(inc): K2, M1, K to last 2 sts, M1, K2. 32 (34: 36: 38: 40: 42) sts.

Work 9 rows, ending with a WS row.

Inc 1 st as before at each end of next row and 3 foll 10th rows, and then on 3 foll 8th rows. 46 (48: 50: 52: 54: 56) sts.

Work straight until sleeves measures 46 (47: 48: 49: 50: 51)cm from cast on edge, ending with a WS row.

Shape sleeve top

Cast off 3 sts at beg of next 2 rows. 40 (42: 44: 46: 48: 50) sts.

Dec 1 st at each end of next 3 rows, then on foll alt row, and then on every foll 4th row to 28 (28: 30: 32: 32: 34) sts, ending with a RS row.

Work 1 row.

Dec 1 st at each end of next row and 3 (2: 1: 3: 1: 2) foll alt rows, and then on every foll row to 14 (16: 16: 18: 18: 18) sts. Cast off.

MAKING UP

Pin the pieces out and steam very gently.

Neck edging

Join the right shoulder sts firmly together. With RS facing and using 5 ½ mm (US 9) needles, pick up and knit 21 sts down left front neck, 22 (22: 26: 28: 30: 34) sts across centre, 21 sts up right front neck, 15 sts down right back neck, 22 (22: 26: 28: 30: 34) sts across back and 15 sts up left back neck. 116 (116: 124: 128: 132: 140) sts.

Beg with purl row, work 2 rows in st st.

Change to 5mm (US 8) needles and work a further 4 rows in st st.

Change to 4 ½ mm (US 7) needles and work a further 5 rows in st st.

Cast off.

Join left shoulder and neck edge seam, reversing the seam on the last 6 rows.

Join side and sleeve seams.

Set sleeve into armhole.

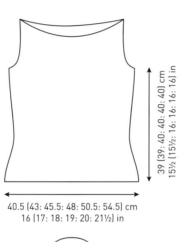

40.5 (43: 45.5: 48: 50.5: 54.5) cm
16 (17: 18: 19: 20: 21½) in

39 (39: 40: 40: 40: 40) cm
15½ (15½: 16: 16: 16: 16) in

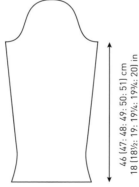

46 (47: 48: 49: 50: 51) cm
18 (18½: 19: 19¼: 19¾: 20) in

PRECIOUS

BEAUTIFUL BEADED CARDIGAN WITH OPTIONAL KNITTED TIE

Recommendation

Suitable for the knitter with a little experience.
Please see pages 12 & 13 for photographs.

	XS	S	M	L	XL	XXL	
To fit	81	86	91	97	101	109	cm
bust	32	34	36	38	40	43	ins

Rowan Kidsilk Haze

3	3	4	4	4	5 x 25gm

Beads

1,000 beads

Ribbon (optional) Approx. 1 metre

Needles

1 pair 3mm (no 11) (US 2) needles
1 pair 3 ¼ mm (no 10) (US 3) needles
1 pair 3mm (no 11) (US 2) double-pointed
needles (for ties only)

Tension

25 sts and 34 rows to 10 cm measured over
pattern using 3 ¼ mm (US 3) needles

Special abbreviation

Bead 1 – see information page for details

BACK

Thread approx. 150 beads onto yarn, as
described on the information page (break
yarn and thread on more beads as necessary).
Cast on 91 (97: 103: 109: 115: 125) sts using
3mm (US 2) needles and **the cable method,**
making sure that the cast-on edge is not at
all tight.
Row 1 (RS): K1, (P1, K1) to end.
Row 2: K1, *place bead as folls: with yarn
at **RS** of work, slip bead up next to st just
worked, slip next st purlwise from left needle
to right needle, K1; rep from * to end.
Row 3: K1, (P1, K1) to end.
Row 4: Purl.
Change to 3 ¼ mm (US 3) needles.
Beg with a K row, work 6 rows in st st.
Row 1 (RS): K3 (6: 3: 6: 3: 2), bead 1, *K5,
bead 1; rep from * to last 3 (6: 3: 6: 3: 2) sts,
K3 (6: 3: 6: 3: 2).
Row 2 and every foll alt row: Purl.
Rows 3, 5 & 7: Knit.
Row 9 (RS) (inc): K2, M1, K4 (1: 4: 1: 4: 3),
bead 1, *K5, bead 1; rep from * to last 6 (3:
6: 3: 6: 5) sts, K4 (1: 4: 1: 4: 3) sts, M1, K2.
93 (99: 105: 111: 117: 127) sts.
Rows 11, 13 & 15: Knit.
Row 16: Purl.
These 16 rows form bead pattern and start
side seam shaping.
Keeping patt correct throughout, work 6 rows.
Inc 1 st at each end of next row and 2 foll
14th rows, taking extra stitches into patt
and ending with a RS row.
99 (105: 111: 117: 123: 133) sts.
Cont straight for a further 11 (11: 13: 15:
19: 19) rows, ending with a WS row.
(Work should meas 21 (21: 21.5: 22: 23: 23)cm.)
Shape armholes
Cast off 6 sts at beg of next 2 rows.
87 (93: 99: 105: 111: 121) sts.
Dec 1 st at each end of next 3 (3: 3: 3: 5: 5)
rows, then on foll 3 (3: 4: 5: 4: 6) alt rows.
75 (81: 85: 89: 93: 99) sts.
Cont straight for a further 49 (51: 49: 49:
53: 53) rows, ending with a WS row.

(Armhole should measure 18 (18.5: 18.5:
19: 20: 21)cm.)
Shape shoulders and back neck
Cast off 8 (8: 8: 9: 9: 10) sts at beg of next
2 rows. 59 (65: 69: 71: 75: 79) sts.
Next row (RS): Cast off 7 (8: 8: 8: 9: 9) sts,
patt until there are 11 (11: 12: 12: 12: 13) sts
on right needle and turn, leaving rem sts on
a holder.
Work each side of neck separately.
Cast off 4 sts at beg of next row.
Cast off rem 7 (7: 8: 8: 8: 9) sts.
With RS facing, rejoin yarn to rem sts, cast off
centre 23 (27: 29: 31: 33: 35) sts, patt to end.
Complete to match first side rev shaping.

LEFT FRONT

**Thread approx 150 beads onto yarn.
Cast on 45 (49: 51: 55: 57: 63) sts using
3mm (US 2) needles and **the cable method,**
making sure that the cast-on edge is not at
all tight.
Row 1 (RS): K1, (P1, K1) to end.
Row 2: K1, * Bead 1, K1; rep from * to end.
Row 3: K1, (P1, K1) to end.
Row 4: Purl across row, inc 1 st at side edge
of row on **XS, M & XL sizes.**
46 (49: 52: 55: 58: 63) sts.
Change to 3 ¼ mm (US 3) needles.
Beg with a K row, work 6 rows in st st. **
Row 1 (RS): K3 (6: 3: 6: 3: 2), bead 1, *K5,
bead 1; rep from * to last 6 sts, K6.
Row 2 and every foll alt row: Purl.
Rows 3, 5 & 7: Knit.
Row 9 (RS) (inc): K2, M1, K4 (1: 4: 1: 4: 3),
bead 1, *K5, bead 1; rep from * to last 3 sts,
K3. 47 (50: 53: 56: 59: 64) sts.
Rows 11, 13 & 15: Knit.
Row 16: Purl.
These 16 rows form bead pattern and start
side seam shaping.
Keeping patt correct throughout, work 6 rows.
Inc 1 st at beg of next row and foll 14th row,
taking extra stitches into patt and ending with
a **RS** row. 49 (52: 55: 58: 61: 66) sts.
Work 1 (1: 3: 5: 5: 5) rows, ending with a WS row.

Shape front neck

Dec 1 st at neck edge on next row and 2 (2: 2: 1: 1: 1) foll 4th rows.

46 (49: 52: 56: 59: 64) sts.

Work 3 (3: 1: 3: 3: 3) rows.

XS, S, L, XL & XXL sizes only

Next row: K2, M1, patt to last 2 sts, K2tog.

46 (49: -: 56: 59: 64) sts.

Med size only

Next row: K2, M1, patt to end. 53 sts.

All sizes

Cont dec at front edge on every 4th row from last dec, work a further 11 (11: 13: 15: 19: 19) rows, ending with a WS row.

44 (47: 50: 53: 55: 60) sts.

Shape armhole

Next row: Cast off 6 sts, patt to last 2 sts, K2tog. 37 (40: 43: 46: 48: 53) sts.

Work 1 row.

Cont dec at neck edge on every 4th row **and at the same time** dec 1 st at armhole edge on next 3 (3: 3: 3: 5: 5) rows, then on foll 3 (3: 4: 5: 4: 6) alt rows. 29 (32: 33: 35: 36: 38) sts.

Cont dec at neck edge on every 4th row to 28 (29: 28: 28: 30: 32) sts, ending with a **RS** row.

Work 5 rows.

Dec 1 st at neck edge on next row and every foll 6th row to 22 (23: 24: 25: 26: 28) sts, ending with a **RS** row.

Work 11 (5: 5: 5: 7: 7) rows.

Shape shoulder

Cast off 8 (8: 8: 9: 9: 10) sts at beg of next row and 7 (8: 8: 8: 9: 9) sts at beg of foll alt row.

Work 1 row.

Cast off rem 7 (7: 8: 8: 8: 9) sts.

RIGHT FRONT

Work for left front from ** to **.

Row 1 (RS): K6, bead 1, *K5, bead 1; rep from * to last 3 (6: 3: 6: 3: 2) sts, K3 (6: 3: 6: 3: 2).

Row 2 and every foll alt row: Purl.

Rows 3, 5 & 7: Knit.

Row 9 (RS): K3, bead 1, *K5, bead 1; rep from * to last 6 (3: 6: 3: 6: 5) sts, K4 (1: 4: 1: 4: 3), M1, K2. 47 (50: 53: 56: 59: 64) sts.

Rows 11, 13 & 15: Knit.

Row 16: Purl.

These 16 rows form bead pattern and start side seam shaping.

Complete as given for left front reversing pattern and all shaping.

SLEEVES (both alike)

Thread approx 150 beads onto yarn (break yarn and thread on more beads as necessary).

Cast on 69 (73: 73: 77: 81: 85) sts using 3mm (US 2) needles and **the cable method**, making sure that the cast-on is not at all tight.

Row 1 (RS): K1, (P1, K1) to end.

Row 2: K1, * Bead 1, K1; rep from * to end.

Row 3: K1, (P1, K1) to end.

Row 4: Purl.

Change to 3 ¼ mm (US 3) needles.

Beg with a K row, work 6 rows in st st.

Row 1 (RS)(inc): K2, M1, K5 (1: 1: 3: 5: 1), bead 1, *K5, bead 1; rep from * to last 7 (3: 3: 5: 7: 3) sts, K5 (1: 1: 3: 5: 1), M1, K2.

71 (75: 75: 79: 83: 87) sts.

Row 2 and every foll alt row: Purl.

Rows 3 & 5: Knit.

Row 7 (RS)(inc): K2, M1, K to last 2 sts, M1, K2.

73 (77: 77: 81: 85: 89) sts.

Row 9: K6 (2: 2: 4: 6: 2), bead 1, *K5, bead 1; rep from * to last 6 (2: 2: 4: 6: 2) sts, K6 (2: 2: 4: 6: 2).

Work 1 (3: 3: 5: 7: 7) rows.

(Sleeve should meas approx 6 (6.5: 6.5: 7: 7.5: 7.5)cm.)

Shape sleeve top

Keeping patt correct, cast off 6 sts at beg of next 2 rows.

61 (65: 65: 69: 73: 77) sts.

Dec 1 st at each end of next 3 rows, then on 2 foll alt rows, and then on every foll 4th row to 41 (45: 45: 49: 53: 55) sts.

Work 1 row.

Dec 1 st at each end of next row and 1 (2: 2: 3: 4: 4) foll alt rows, and then on every row until 31 (33: 33: 35: 37: 39) sts, ending with a WS row.

Cast off 3 sts at beg of next 2 rows.

Cast off rem 25 (27: 27: 29: 31: 33) sts.

MAKING UP

Pin the pieces out, pulling gently to the correct size and shape. Using a steam iron, steam the pieces, but **do not** let the iron touch the knitting at all. Leave for a few seconds to cool, then complete as folls:

Use back stitch, or mattress stitch if preferred.

Join the shoulder seams.

Join sleeve and side seams.

Set sleeve top in armhole.

Front edging

Thread approx 113 (115: 117: 121: 127: 135) beads onto yarn.

With RS of right front facing and using 3mm (US 2) needles, starting and ending at cast-on edges, pick up and knit 32 (32: 33: 34: 34: 34) sts up right front opening edge to start of front slope, 64 (66: 66: 68: 72: 76) sts up right front slope to shoulder, 31 (35: 37: 39: 41: 43) sts from back, 64 (66: 66: 68: 72: 76) sts down left front slope to start of front slope shaping, then 32 (32: 33: 34: 34: 34) sts down left front opening edge.

223 (231: 235: 243: 253: 263) sts.

Row 1 (WS): P1, (K1, P1) to end.

Row 2: P1, (bead 1, P1) to end.

Cast off in moss st.

Ties (make 2)

Cast on 3 sts using 3mm (US 2) double pointed needles and knit 1 row.

*Without turning needle, slip sts to opposite end of needle and, taking yarn quite tightly around back of work to prevent a ladder from forming, knit these 3 sts again.

Rep from * until tie measures approx 50cm.

K3tog and fasten off.

Sew on ties/ribbons at centre front opening edge, using photograph as a guide.

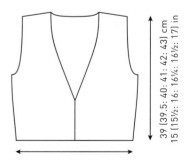

39.5 (42: 44.5: 47: 49.5: 53.5) cm
15½ (16½: 17½: 18½: 19½: 21) in

39 (39.5: 40: 41: 42: 43) cm
15 (15½: 16: 16¼: 16½: 17) in

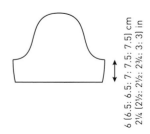

6 (6.5: 6.5: 7: 7.5: 7.5) cm
2¼ (2½: 2½: 2¾: 3: 3) in

CALM

CLOSE FITTING SHEER SWEATER WITH EYELET DETAILS

Recommendation

Suitable for the novice knitter.
Please see pages 14 – 16 for photographs.

	XS	S	M	L	XL	XXL	
To fit	**81**	**86**	**91**	**97**	**102**	**109**	**cm**
bust	32	34	36	38	40	43	in

Rowan Kidsilk Aura

6 6 6 7 7 8 x 25gm

Needles

1 pair 6mm (no 4) (US 10) needles
1 pair 7mm (no 2) (US 10 1/2) needles
1 pair 8mm (no 0) (US 11) needles

Tension

11 sts and 15 rows to 10cm measured over
reversed stocking stitch using 8mm (US 11)
needles

Pattern note:

This is intended to be a very close fitting
sweater, which stretches slightly to fit.

BACK

Cast on 78 (86: 90: 94: 102: 110) sts
using 6mm (US 10) needles.
Change to 8mm (US 11) needles.
Foundation row (RS)(dec): *Sl 1, K1, psso;
rep from * to end.
39 (43: 45: 47: 51: 55) sts.
Next row (WS): Knit.
Beg with a P row, cont in rev st st, shaping
sides as folls:
Work 10 rows.
Next row (RS)(dec): P2, P2tog, P to last
4 sts, P2tog tbl, P2.
37 (41: 43: 45: 49: 53) sts.
Work 7 rows.
Dec 1 st as before at each end of next row
and foll 8th row, ending with a **RS** row.
33 (37: 39: 41: 45: 49) sts.
Work 11 rows.
Next row (RS)(inc): P2, M1p, P to last
2 sts, M1p, P2.
35 (39: 41: 43: 47: 51) sts.
Work 5 rows, ending with a WS row.
Inc 1 st as before at each end of next row
and 2 foll 6th rows.
41 (45: 47: 49: 53: 57) sts.
Work straight until back measures 44cm,
ending with a WS row.
Shape raglans
Cast off 3 sts at beg of next 2 rows.
35 (39: 41: 43: 47: 51) sts.
Work 2 rows. **
Dec 1 st at each end of next row,
then on 2 (3: 3: 4: 3: 3) foll 4th rows,
and 2 (1: 1: 0: 2: 3) foll alt rows, ending
with a RS row.
25 (29: 31: 33: 35: 37) sts.
Work 1 row.
Cast off.

FRONT

Work as given for back to **.
Dec 1 st at each end of next row, then on
1 (2: 2: 2: 2: 2) foll 4th rows, ending with
a RS row.
Work 3 (1: 1: 3: 3: 3) rows.

Shape front neck

XS, L, XL & XXL sizes only
Next row (RS): P2tog, P until there are
4 (·: ·: 3: 4: 7) sts on right needle and turn,
leaving rem sts on a holder.
Work each side of neck separately.
Dec 1 st at neck edge, work to end.
3 (·: ·: 2: 3: 6) sts.
Dec 1 (·: ·: 0: 1: 1) st at beg and 1 (·: ·: 1: 1:
1) st at end of next row, then for **XXL size
only,** rep last 2 rows once more.
1 (·: ·: 1: 1: 1) st.
Work 1 row.
Fasten off.
S & M sizes only
Purl until 4 sts on on right needle and turn,
leaving rem sts on a holder.
Work each side of neck separately.
Dec 1 st at neck edge, work to end. 3 sts.
Dec 1 st at each end of next row. 1 st.
Work 1 row.
Fasten off.
With RS facing and using 8mm (US 11)
needles, cast off centre 21 (25: 27: 29: 31:
29) sts, work to end.
Complete to match first side rev shaping.

SLEEVES (work both the same)

Cast on 40 (44: 44: 52: 52: 56) sts using
6mm (US 10) needles.
Change to 8mm (US 11) needles.
Foundation row (RS)(dec): *Sl 1, K1, psso;
rep from * to end. 20 (22: 22: 26: 26: 28) sts.
Next row (WS): Knit.
Beg with a P row, cont in **rev st st**, shaping
sides as folls:
Work 12 rows, ending with a WS row.
Next row (RS)(inc): P2, M1p, P to last 2 sts,
M1p, P2. 22 (24: 24: 28: 28: 30) sts.
Work 13 rows.
Inc 1 st as before at each end of next row,
then on foll 14th row and then on 2 foll 12th
rows. 30 (32: 32: 36: 36: 38) sts.
Work straight until sleeve measures 49 (50:
51: 52: 53: 54)cm from cast on edge, ending
with a WS row.

Shape raglan

Cast off 3 sts at beg of next 2 rows.
24 (26: 26: 30: 30: 32) sts.
Work 2 rows.
Dec 1 st at each end of next row and
2 (3: 3: 3: 3: 4) foll 4th rows and then
on 1 (0: 0: 1: 1: 0) foll alt row, ending
with **a RS** row.
16 (18: 18: 20: 20: 22) sts.

Shape top
Left sleeve only

Cast off 7 (9: 9: 9: 9: 10) sts, K to end.
Dec 1 st at beg of next row.
Cast off rem 8 (8: 8: 10: 10: 11) sts.

Right sleeve only

Work 1 row.
Cast off 7 (9: 9: 9: 9: 10) sts at beg
and dec 1 st at end of next row.
8 (8: 8: 10: 10: 11) sts.
Work 1 row.
Cast off.

MAKING UP

Pin the pieces out pulling gently into shape
and steam gently.
Join 3 raglan seams leaving the back left
seam open.

Neck edging

With RS facing and using 7mm (US 10 ½)
needles, pick up and knit 15 (17: 17:
19: 19: 21) sts across left sleeve top,
27 (31: 33: 35: 37: 39) sts across front,
15 (17: 17: 19: 19: 21) sts across right
sleeve top and 25 (29: 31: 33: 35: 37) sts
across back.
82 (94: 98: 106: 110: 118) sts.
Next row (WS): Purl.
Change to 6mm (US 10) needles.
Row 1: K1, (yfwd, sl 1, K1, psso) to last st, K1.
Row 2: Work as row 1.
Beg with a K row work 4 rows in st st, ending
with a WS row.
Cast off.
Join rem raglan and neck edging seam.
Join side and sleeve seams.

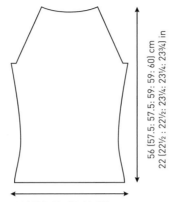

56 (57.5: 57.5: 59: 59: 60) cm
22 (22½ : 22½: 23¼: 23¼: 23¾) in

38 (40.5: 43: 45: 48: 52) cm
15 (16: 17: 18: 19: 20½) in

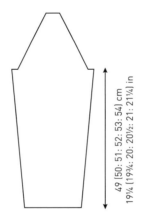

49 (50: 51: 52: 53: 54) cm
19¼ (19¾: 20: 20½: 21: 21¼) in

DARCY

FITTED PEPLUM JACKET WITH A TOUCH OF THE EQUESTRIAN

Recommendation
Suitable for the more experienced knitter.
Please see pages 17 – 19 for photographs.

	XS	S	M	L	XL	XXL	
To fit	81	86	91	97	102	109	cm
bust	32	34	36	38	40	43	in

Rowan Handknit Cotton

| 13 | 13 | 14 | 15 | 16 | 17 | x 50gm |

Needles
1 pair 3 ¼mm (no 10) (US 3) needles
1 pair 4mm (no 8) (US 6) needles

Buttons 9

Tension
20 sts and 30 rows to 10cm measured over
moss stitch using 4mm (US 6) needles

**Pattern note (flounce edging on back and
fronts):** When starting next set of sts in moss
st after each rev st st panel, always start with
the same type of st as that used for the last
st of the previous panel – i.e. if the previous
section ends with "K1", start the next section
of moss st with "K1" as well.

BACK
Cast on 127 (133: 137: 153: 157: 165)
sts using 4mm (US 6) needles and work
flounce and shape lower edge, setting
sts as folls:
Short row shaping rows 1 & 2: Moss st
17 (20: 22: 23: 25: 29), P13 (13: 13: 15:
15: 15), now starting with the **same** type of
st as that used for the last st of the previous
moss st panel (see patt note) moss st 9 (9: 9:
11: 11: 11), P13 (13: 13: 15: 15: 15), again
starting with the same type of st as that used
for the last st of previous moss st panel moss
st 23 (23: 23: 25: 25: 25), wrap next st (by
slipping next st onto right needle, taking yarn
to opposite side of work between needles and
then slipping same st back onto left needle)
and turn, moss st 23 (23: 23: 25: 25: 25),
wrap next st and turn.
Short row shaping rows 3 & 4: Moss st 23
(23: 23: 25: 25: 25), P13 (13: 13: 15: 15:
15), moss st 9 (9: 9: 11: 11: 11), wrap next
st and turn, moss st 9 (9: 9: 11: 11: 11), K13
(13: 13: 15: 15: 15), moss st 23 (23: 23: 25:
25: 25), K13 (13: 13: 15: 15: 15), moss st 9
(9: 9: 11: 11: 11), wrap next st and turn.
Short row shaping rows 5 & 6: Moss st 9
(9: 9: 11: 11: 11), P13 (13: 13: 15: 15: 15),
moss st 23 (23: 23: 25: 25: 25), P13 (13:
13: 15: 15: 15), moss st 9 (9: 9: 11: 11: 11),
P13 (13: 13: 15: 15: 15), moss st 7 (7: 7: 9:
9: 9), wrap next st and turn, moss st 7 (7: 7:
9: 9: 9), K13 (13: 13: 15: 15: 15), moss st 9
(9: 9: 11: 11: 11), K13 (13: 13: 15: 15: 15),
moss st 23 (23: 23: 25: 25: 25), K13 (13: 13:
15: 15: 15), moss st 9 (9: 9: 11: 11: 11), K13
(13: 13: 15: 15: 15), moss st 7 (7: 7: 9: 9: 9),
wrap next st and turn.

Short row shaping rows 7 & 8: Moss st
7 (7: 7: 9: 9: 9), P13 (13: 13: 15: 15: 15),
moss st 9 (9: 9: 11: 11: 11), P13 (13: 13:
15: 15: 15), moss st 23 (23: 23: 25: 25: 25),
P13 (13: 13: 15: 15: 15), moss st 9 (9: 9: 11:
11: 11), P13 (13: 13: 15: 15: 15), moss st
15 (15: 15: 17: 17: 17), wrap next st and
turn, moss st 15 (15: 15: 17: 17: 17), K13
(13: 13: 15: 15: 15), moss st 9 (9: 9: 11: 11:
11), K13 (13: 13: 15: 15: 15), moss st 23
(23: 23: 25: 25: 25), K13 (13: 13: 15: 15:
15), moss st 9 (9: 9: 11: 11: 11), K13 (13:
13: 15: 15: 15), moss st 15 (15: 15: 17:
17: 17), wrap next st and turn.
Row 9 (RS): Moss st 15 (15: 15: 17: 17:
17), P13 (13: 13: 15: 15: 15), moss st
9 (9: 9: 11: 11: 11), P13 (13: 13: 15: 15: 15),
moss st 23 (23: 23: 25: 25: 25), P13 (13: 13:
15: 15: 15), moss st 9 (9: 9: 11: 11: 11),
P13 (13: 13: 15: 15: 15), moss st to end.
Row 10: Moss st 17 (20: 22: 23: 25: 29),
K13 (13: 13: 15: 15: 15), moss st 9 (9: 9:
11: 11: 11), K13 (13: 13: 15: 15: 15), moss
st 23 (23: 23: 25: 25: 25), K13 (13: 13: 15:
15: 15), moss st 9 (9: 9: 11: 11: 11), K13
(13: 13: 15: 15: 15), moss st to end.
The last 2 rows set the sts for the flounce.
Place a marker on the needle at each side
of the 4 rev st st panels. Slip the markers
from left to right needle on next and every foll
row up to top of flounce.
Keeping sts correct cont as folls: Work 2 rows.
Row 1 (RS)(dec): *Patt to next marker, P2tog,
P to 2 sts before next marker, P2tog tbl; rep
from * 3 times more, patt to end.
119 (125: 129: 145: 149: 157) sts.
Work 3 rows.
Row 5: Dec 1 st at each end of next row.
117 (123: 127: 143: 147: 155) sts.
Work 5 rows.
Row 11 (RS)(dec): Patt 2tog, *patt to next
marker, P2tog, P to 2 sts before next marker,
P2tog tbl; rep from * 3 times more, patt to
last 2 sts, patt 2tog.
107 (113: 117: 133: 137: 145) sts.
Work 3 rows.

Row 15: Work as row 5. 105 (111: 115: 131: 135: 143) sts.
Work 3 rows.
Row 19 (RS)(dec): Work as row 11.
95 (101: 105: 121: 125: 133) sts.
Work 3 rows.
Row 23: Work as row 5.
93 (99: 103: 119: 123: 131) sts.
Work 1 row.
Dec 1 st as before at each side of the **rev st st** panels on next row and 1 (1: 1: 2: 2: 2) foll 4th rows and **at the same time** cont to dec 1 st at each end of next 1 (1: 1: 2: 2: 2) foll 4th rows. 75 (81: 85: 91: 95: 103) sts.
Work 1 row.
Next row (RS)(dec): Patt 2tog, *patt to next marker, patt 3tog; rep from * 3 times more, patt to last 2 sts, patt 2tog.
65 (71: 75: 81: 85: 93) sts.
Work 3 rows.
Dec 1 st at each end of next row.
63 (69: 73: 79: 83: 91) sts.
Work 3 rows, ending with a WS row.
Place a marker at each end of last row.
Keeping patt correct cont in moss st, shaping sides as folls:
Work 10 rows, ending with a WS row.
Inc 1 st at each end of next row.
65 (71: 75: 81: 85: 93) sts.
Work 7 rows.
Inc 1 st at each end of next row and then on every foll 6th row to 81 (87: 91: 97: 101: 109) sts.
Work straight until back measures 23 (23: 24: 24: 24: 24)cm from markers, ending with a WS row.
Shape armholes
Cast off 4 sts at beg of next 2 rows. 73 (79: 83: 89: 93: 101) sts.
Dec 1 st at each end of next 3 rows, then on 2 (2: 2: 3: 3: 4) foll alt rows and then on 1 (2: 2: 2: 2: 2) foll 4th rows.
61 (65: 69: 73: 77: 83) sts.
Work straight until armhole measures 18 (19: 19: 20: 21: 22)cm, ending with a WS row.
Shape shoulders and back neck
Cast off 5 (6: 6: 6: 6: 7) sts at beg of next 2 rows. 51 (53: 57: 61: 65: 69) sts.
Cast off 5 (5: 6: 6: 6: 7) sts, patt until there are 9 (9: 9: 10: 11: 11) sts on right needle and turn, leaving rem sts on a holder.
Work each side of neck separately.
Cast off 4 sts work to end.
Cast off rem 5 (5: 5: 6: 7: 7) sts.

With RS facing rejoin yarn to rem sts, cast off centre 23 (25: 27: 29: 31: 33) sts, patt to end. Complete to match first side, reversing shaping.

LEFT FRONT
Cast on 67 (70: 72: 80: 82: 86) sts using 4mm (US 6) needles and work flounce and shape lower edge, setting sts as folls:
Short row shaping rows 1 & 2 (RS): Moss st 4 (7: 9: 5: 7: 11), wrap next st and turn, moss st to end.
Short row shaping rows 3 & 4: Moss st 10 (13: 15: 13: 15: 19), wrap next st and turn, moss st to end.
Short row shaping rows 5 & 6: Moss st 17 (20: 22: 23: 25: 29), wrap next st and turn, moss st to end.
Row 7 (RS): Moss st 17 (20: 22: 23: 25: 29), P11 (11: 11: 13: 13: 13), moss st 9 (9: 9: 11: 11: 11), P11 (11: 11: 13: 13: 13), moss st 19 (19: 19: 20: 20: 20).
Row 8: Moss st 19 (19: 19: 20: 20: 20), K11 (11: 11: 13: 13: 13), moss st 9 (9: 9: 11: 11: 11), K11 (11: 11: 13: 13: 13), moss to end.
The last 2 rows set the sts for the flounce.
Dec 1 st at beg of next row.
66 (69: 71: 79: 81: 85) sts.
Work 5 rows.
Place a marker on the needle at each side of the 2 rev st st panels.
Slip the markers from left to right needle on next and every foll row up to top of flounce.
Row 1 (RS)(dec): Patt 2tog, *patt to next marker, P2tog, P to 2 sts before next marker, P2tog tbl; rep from * once more, patt to end.
61 (64: 66: 74: 76: 80) sts.
Work 3 rows.
Row 5: Dec 1 st at beg of next row.
60 (63: 65: 73: 75: 79) sts.
Work 3 rows.
Row 9 (RS)(dec): Work as row 1.
55 (58: 60: 68: 70: 74) sts.
Work 3 rows.
Row 13: Work as row 5.
54 (57: 59: 67: 69: 73) sts.
Work 1 row.
Dec 1 st as before at each side of the rev st st panels on next row and 1 (1: 1: 2: 2: 2) foll 4th rows and at the same time cont to dec 1 st at side edge on every 4th row from last dec.
Work 1 row.

Next row (RS)(dec): Patt 2tog, *patt to next marker, patt 3tog; rep from * once more, patt to end. 40 (43: 45: 48: 50: 54) sts.
Work 1 row.
Dec 1 st at beg of next row.
39 (42: 44: 47: 49: 53) sts.
Work 3 rows, ending with a WS row.
Place a marker at each end of last row.
Keeping patt correct cont in moss st, shaping side as folls:
Work 10 rows, ending with a WS row.
Inc 1 st at beg of next row and foll 8th row and then on every foll 6th row to 48 (51: 53: 56: 58: 62) sts.
Work straight until front matches back to beg of armhole shaping, ending with a WS row.
Shape armhole
Cast off 4 sts at beg of next row.
44 (47: 49: 52: 54: 58) sts.
Work 1 row.
Dec 1 st at armhole edge on next 3 rows, then on 2 (2: 2: 3: 3: 4) foll alt rows and then on 1 (2: 2: 2: 2: 2) foll 4th rows.
38 (40: 42: 44: 46: 49) sts.
Work straight until front is 10 (10: 12: 12: 14: 14) rows shorter than back to shoulder shaping, ending with a WS row.
Shape front neck
Next row (RS): Patt 21 (22: 24: 25: 27: 30) sts and turn, leaving rem 17 (18: 18: 19: 19: 19) sts on a holder for neck edging.
Dec 1 st at neck edge on next 4 (4: 4: 4: 4: 6) rows, then on 2 (2: 3: 3: 4: 3) foll alt rows.
15 (16: 17: 18: 19: 21) sts.
Work 1 row, ending with a WS row.
Shape shoulder
Cast off 5 (6: 6: 6: 6: 7) sts at beg of next row and 5 (5: 6: 6: 6: 7) sts at beg of foll alt row.
Work 1 row.
Cast off rem 5 (5: 5: 6: 7: 7) sts.
Mark position of 9 buttons, the first to come on row after marked row at waistline, the 9th to come 4 rows down from neck edge and rem 7 spaced evenly between.

RIGHT FRONT
Cast on 67 (70: 72: 80: 82: 86) sts using 4mm (US 6) needles and work flounce and shape lower edge, setting sts as folls:
Row 1 (RS): Moss st 19 (19: 19: 20: 20: 20), P11 (11: 11: 13: 13: 13), moss st 9 (9: 9: 11: 11: 11), P11 (11: 11: 13: 13: 13), moss st 17 (20: 22: 23: 25: 29).

Short row shaping rows 2 & 3 (RS): Moss st 4 (7: 9: 5: 7: 11), wrap next st and turn, moss st to end.

Short row shaping rows 4 & 5: Moss st 10 (13: 15: 13: 15: 19), wrap next st and turn, moss st to end.

Short row shaping rows 6 & 7: Moss st 17 (20: 22: 23: 25: 29), wrap next st and turn, moss st to end.

Row 8 (WS): Moss st 17 (20: 22: 23: 25: 29), K11 (11: 11: 13: 13: 13), moss st 9 (9: 9: 11: 11: 11), K11 (11: 11: 13: 13: 13), moss st 19 (19: 19: 20: 20: 20) sts.

The last 2 rows set the sts for the flounce.

Dec 1 st at end of next row.

66 (69: 71: 79: 81: 85) sts.

Work 5 rows.

Place a marker on the needle at each side of the 2 rev st st panels.

Slip the markers from left to right needle on next and every foll row up to top of flounce.

Row 1 (RS)(dec): *Patt to next marker, P2tog, P to 2 sts before next marker, P2tog tbl; rep from * once more, patt to last 2 sts, patt 2tog.

61 (64: 66: 74: 76: 80) sts.

Work 3 rows.

Row 5: Dec 1 st at end of next row.

60 (63: 65: 73: 75: 79) sts.

Work 3 rows.

Row 9 (RS)(dec): Work as row 1.

55 (58: 60: 68: 70: 74) sts.

Work 3 rows.

Row 13: Work as row 5.

54 (57: 59: 67: 69: 73) sts.

Work 1 row.

Dec 1 st as before at each side of the **rev st st** panels on next row and 1 (1: 1: 2: 2: 2) foll 4th rows and **at the same time** cont to dec 1 st at side edge on every 4th row from last dec.

Work 1 row.

Next row (RS)(dec): *Patt to next marker, patt 3tog; rep from * once more, patt to last 2 sts, patt 2tog. 40 (43: 45: 48: 50: 54) sts.

Work 1 row.

Dec 1 st at end of next row.

39 (42: 44: 47: 49: 53) sts.

Work 3 rows, ending with a WS row.

Place a marker at each end of last row.

Next row (RS)(buttonhole): Patt 5 sts, patt 2tog, yon, patt to end.

Work 1 row.

Keeping patt correct cont in moss st, shaping side as folls:

Work 8 rows, ending with a WS row. Complete to match left front, rev shapings and working buttonholes as before to correspond with positions marked for buttons.

SLEEVES (work both the same)
Cast on 39 (41: 43: 45: 47: 49) sts using 4mm (US 6) needles.

Row 1 (RS): K1, (P1, K1) to end.

Row 2: Work as row 1.

These 2 rows form **moss st.**

Cont in moss st working shaping as folls:

Work a further 10 rows.

Inc 1 st at each end of next row and 6 (6: 6: 2: 2: 2) foll 12th rows.

53 (55: 57: 51: 53: 55) sts.

Work 13 rows.

Inc 1 st at each end of next row and then on every foll 14th row to 59 (61: 63: 65: 67: 69) sts.

Work straight until sleeve measures 45 (46: 47: 48: 49: 50) cm, ending with a WS row.

Shape sleeve top
Cast off 4 sts at beg of next 2 rows.

51 (53: 55: 57: 59: 61) sts.

Dec 1 st at each end of next 3 rows, then on foll alt row and then on every foll 4th row to 31 (33: 35: 35: 37: 37) sts, ending with a RS row.

Work 1 row.

Dec 1 st at each end of next row and 1 (2: 3: 2: 3: 3) foll alt rows, and then on every foll row to 17 (17: 17: 19: 19: 19) sts. Cast off.

MAKING UP
Press all pieces as described on the information page.

Join shoulder seams, using back stitch or mattress st if preferred.

Neck edging
With RS of right front facing and using 4mm (US 6) needles, slip 17 (18: 18: 19: 19: 19) sts from holder onto right needle, rejoin yarn and pick up and knit 10 (10: 12: 12: 14: 14) sts up right front neck, 31 (33: 35: 37: 39: 41) sts across back and 10 (10: 12: 12: 14: 14) sts down left front neck, work in moss st across 17 (18: 18: 19: 19: 19) on holder.

85 (89: 95: 99: 105: 107) sts.

Place a marker on first and last st of back neck sts.

Cont in moss st as folls:

Work 1 row.

Next row (RS)(dec): Patt to 1 st before marked st , patt 3tog, patt to 1 st before second marked stitch, patt 3tog, patt to end.

81 (85: 91: 95: 101: 103) sts.

Work 3 rows.

Change to 3 ¼ mm (US 3) needles.

Dec 4 sts as before on next row and foll 4th row.

73 (77: 83: 87: 93: 95) sts.

Work 4 rows, ending with a RS row.

Cast off in patt.

Join side and sleeve seams.

Set sleeves into armholes.

Sew on buttons to correspond with buttonholes.

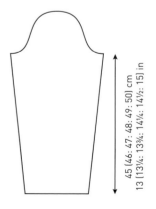

40.5 (43: 45.5: 48: 50.5: 54) cm
16 (17: 18: 19: 20: 21½) in

41 (42: 43: 44: 45: 46) cm
16 (16½: 17: 17¼: 17¾: 18) in

45 (46: 47: 48: 49: 50) cm
13 (13¾: 13¾: 14¼: 14½: 15) in

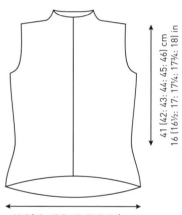

GEM
CHIC CROCHET BERET WITH BEADED TRIM

Recommendation

Suitable for average ability.
Please see pages 10 & 11 for photographs.

Rowan Kid Classic & Kidsilk Haze

| Kid Classic | 1 | x 50gm |
| Kidsilk Haze | 1 | x 25gm |

Beads 300

Crochet hook

6mm (no 4) (US J10)

Tension

11 trebles to 10cm using 6mm (no 4)
(US J10) crochet hook and one strand each of
Kid Classic and Kidsilk Haze

Special abbreviations

Tr2tog = * wrap the yarn over the hook, insert
the hook into the next stitch, wrap the yarn,
draw a loop through, wrap the yarn and draw
through 2 of the loops on the hook (2 loops
left on the hook). Repeat from * into the
following stitch (3 loops on the hook). Wrap
yarn and draw it through all loops.

BERET

Using 6mm (no 4) (US J10) crochet hook and
one strand each of Kid Classic and Kidsilk
Haze, work 4 ch, ss into first chain to form a circle.
Round 1: 3 ch (counts as tr), work 17 tr into
circle, ss into top of 3ch. 18sts.
Round 2 (inc): 3 ch (counts as tr), 2 tr into
next stitch, *1 tr into next stitch, 2 tr into next
stitch; rep from * 7 times more, ss into top
of 3ch. 27 sts.
Round 3 (inc): 3 ch (counts as tr), 1 tr into
next stitch, 2 tr into next stitch, *1 tr into each
of next 2 stitches, 2 tr into next stitch; rep from
* 7 times more, ss into top of 3ch. 36 sts.
Round 4 (inc): 3 ch (counts as tr), 1 tr into
each of next 2 stitches, 2 tr into next stitch,
*1 tr into each of next 3 stitches, 2 tr into
next stitch; rep from * 7 times more, ss into
top of 3 ch. 45 sts.
Round 5 (inc): 3 ch (counts as tr), 1 tr into
each of next 3 stitches, 2 tr into next stitch,
*1 tr into each of next 4 sts, 2 tr into next
stitch; rep from * 7 times more, ss into top
of 3 ch. 54 sts.
Round 6 (inc): 3 ch (counts as tr), 1 tr into
each of next 4 sts, 2 tr into next stitch, *1
tr into each of next 5 stitches, 2 tr into next
stitch; rep from * 7 times more, ss into top
of 3 ch. 63 sts.
Round 7 (inc): 3 ch (counts as tr), 1 tr into
each of next 5 sts, 2 tr into next stitch, *1
tr into each of next 6 stitches, 2 tr into next
stitch; rep from * 7 times more, ss into top
of 3 ch. 72 sts.
Round 8 (inc): 3 ch (counts as tr), 1 tr into
each of next 6 sts, 2 tr into next stitch, *1
tr into each of next 7 stitches, 2 tr into next
stitch; rep from * 7 times more, ss into top of
3 ch. 81 sts.
Round 9 (inc): 3 ch (counts as tr), 1 tr into
each of next 7 sts, 2 tr into next stitch, *1
tr into each of next 8 stitches, 2 tr into next
stitch; rep from * 7 times more, ss into top of
3 ch. 90 sts.
Round 10: 3 ch (counts as tr), 1 tr into every
st to end, ss into top of 3 ch.
Round 11 (dec): 3 ch (counts as tr), 1 tr into
next 7 sts, tr2tog, *1 tr into next 8 sts, tr2tog;
rep from * 7 times more, ss into top of 3 ch.
81 sts.
Round 12 (dec): 3 ch (counts as tr), 1 tr into
next 6 sts, tr2tog, *1 tr into next 7 sts, tr2tog;
rep from * 7 times more, ss into top of 3 ch.
72 sts.
Round 13 (dec): 3 ch (counts as tr), 1 tr into
next 5 sts, tr2tog, *1 tr into next 6 sts, tr2tog;
rep from * 7 times more, ss into top of 3 ch.
63 sts.
Round 14 (dec): 3 ch (counts as tr), 1 tr into
next 4 sts, tr2tog, *1 tr into next 5 sts, tr2tog;
rep from * 7 times more, ss into top of 3 ch.
54 sts.
Round 15: 2ch (counts as htr), 1 htr into
every st to end, ss into top of 2 ch.
Round 16: Work as round 15.
Break the strand of Kidsilk Haze and thread
approximately 100 beads onto this yarn.
Beaded band
Rejoin yarn and cont as folls:
Round 17: 1 ch (counts as dc), *bring a bead
up to about 1·2 cm from hook, 1 dc into next
st easing the bead to the front of the work;
rep from * to end, ss into top of 2 ch.
Rep the last round 4 times more, breaking
yarn and threading further beads on as
required.
Break off the Kid Classic and join two more
ends of Kidsilk Haze and work as folls:
Finishing round: Using 3 strands of Kidsilk
Haze, without turning, 1dc back into last st
worked on previous round, * 1dc into next
stitch to right; rep from * to end.
Fasten off.

WARD

A DOUBLE BUTTONED SLEEVELESS CARDIGAN

Recommendation

Suitable for the knitter with a little experience.
Please see pages 20 & 21 for photographs.

	XS	S	M	L	XL	XXL	
To fit	81	86	91	97	102	109	cm
bust	32	34	36	38	40	43	in

Rowan Kid Classic

| | 5 | 5 | 5 | 6 | 6 | 7 | x 50gm |

Needles

1 pair 4mm (no 8) (US 6) needles
1 pair 4 ½ mm (no 7) (US 7) needles

Buttons 2

Tension

21 sts and 27 rows to 10cm measured over
reversed stocking stitch using 4 ½ mm (US7)
needles

FRONTS & BACK (knitted in one piece)

LEFT FRONT

Cast on 62 (64: 68: 69: 72: 75) sts using
4mm (US 6) needles.
Work edging as folls:
Next row (RS): K0 (1: 0: 1: 0: 0), P1 (2: 2: 2:
1: 0), (K2, P2) to last 29 (29: 30: 30: 31: 31)
sts, place marker on needle before next stitch,
K29 (29: 30: 30: 31: 31) sts for front band.
Next row: Knit to marker, slip marker from
left to right needle (on this row and every foll
row), (K2, P2) to last 1 (3: 2: 3: 1: 0) sts, K1
(2: 2: 2: 1: 0), P0 (1: 0: 1: 0: 0).
These 2 rows set the stitches for the rib
and front band.
Rep the last 2 rows 1 (1: 1: 2: 2: 2) times
more.
Now work front bands in **horizontal rib** as
folls:
Row 1 (RS): Work in rib to marker, K to end.
Row 2: P to marker, rib to end.
Rows 3 & 4: Work as rows 1 & 2.
Row 5: Work in rib to marker, P to end.
Row 6: K to marker, rib to end.
Rows 7 & 8: Work as rows 5 & 6.
These 8 rows form the **horizontal rib** patt for
the front band and are rep up the entire front.
Keeping patt correct, cont on sts as set for
a further 12 rows, ending with patt row 4 of
horizontal rib (WS row).
Change to 4 ½ mm (US 7) needles.
Next row (RS): P to marker, patt to end.
Next row: Patt to marker, K to end.
These 2 rows set the stitches.
Keeping front band patt correct and working
rem sts in **rev st st** cont as folls:
Work 2 rows.
Shape front slope and side edge
Next row (RS)(dec): P to 2 sts before marker,
P2tog, patt to end.
61 (63: 67: 68: 71: 74) sts.
Work 3 rows.
Rep the last 4 rows once more, ending with
a WS row.
60 (62: 66: 67: 70: 73) sts.

Next row (RS)(dec)(inc): P2, M1p, P to 2 sts
before marker, P2tog, patt to end.
60 (62: 66: 67: 70: 73) sts.
Work 3 rows.
Cont dec at front slope on next row, and every
foll 4th row until 6 (8: 7: 9: 11: 10) **front** edge
dec in all have been completed, and then cont
dec on every foll 6th row, and **at the same
time** cont shaping side as folls:
Inc 1 st at side edge on next row and 2 (2: 3:
2: 3: 3) foll 4th rows, then on 4 (4: 3: 4: 3: 3)
foll alt rows, and then on next 9 rows, ending
with a WS row, turn and cast on 10 (10: 10:
11: 11: 12) sts. 81 (82: 86: 88: 90: 94) sts.
Place a second marker 14 (14: 14: 15:
5: 16) sts in from armhole edge.
Keeping front slope shaping correct, and
working 14 (14; 14: 15: 15: 16) sts at
armhole edge in **horizontal rib** to match
front band, cont as folls:
Keeping patt and front shaping correct
cont until 74 (75: 79: 80: 82: 86) sts rem.
Work 13 rows, ending with a WS row.
Place a marker at the armhole edge on
last row to indicate the shoulder line.
Shape back neck
Next row: Work to marker and turn, leaving
rem 29 (29: 30: 30: 31: 31) sts on a holder for
back neck edging. 45 (46: 49: 50: 51: 55) sts.
Work 5 rows, ending with a WS row.
Inc 1 st at neck edge on next row.
Work 3 rows.
Inc 1 st at neck edge on next row and 2 foll alt
rows, and then on 3 foll rows, ending with a
WS row. 52 (53: 56: 57: 58: 62) sts.
Work 1 row. ***
Leave sts on a spare needle.

RIGHT FRONT

Cast on 62 (64: 68: 69: 72: 75) sts using
4mm (US 6) needles.
Work edging as folls:
Next row (RS): K29 (29: 30: 30: 31: 31) sts
for front band, place a marker on needle
before next stitch, (P2, K2) to last 1 (3: 2: 3:
1: 0) sts, P1 (2: 2: 2: 1: 0), K0 (1: 0: 1: 0: 0).

Next row: P0 (1: 0: 1: 0: 0), K1 (2: 2: 2: 1: 0), (P2, K2) to marker, slip marker from left to right needle (on this row and every foll row), K29 (29: 30: 30: 31: 31).
These 2 rows set the stitches for the rib and front band.
Rep the last 2 rows 1 (1: 1: 2: 2: 2) times more.
Now work front bands in **horizontal rib** as folls:
Row 1 (RS): K to marker, rib to end.
Row 2: Rib to marker, P to end.
Rows 3 & 4: Work as rows 1 & 2.
Row 5: P to marker, rib to end.
Row 6: Rib to marker, K to end.
Rows 7 & 8: Work as rows 5 & 6.
These 8 rows form the horizontal rib patt for the front band and are rep up the entire front.
Keeping patt correct, cont on sts as set for a further 10 rows, ending with patt row 2 of **horizontal rib** (WS row).
Next row (RS)(Buttonholes): K7, cast off 3 sts, K until there are 10 (10: 11: 11: 12: 12) sts on needle after those cast off, cast off 3 sts, work to end.
Work 1 row casting on 3 sts over those cast off on previous row.
Change to 4 ½ mm (US 7) needles.
Next row (RS): Patt to marker, P to end.
Next row: K to marker, patt to end.
These 2 rows set the stitches.
Keeping front band patt correct and working rem sts in **rev st st,** complete to match left front reversing all shaping and ending at ***.
52 (53: 56: 57: 58: 62) sts.
Join fronts together
Next row (WS): Patt across right front sts, cast on 34 (36: 36: 38: 40: 40) sts, patt across 52 (53: 56: 57: 58: 62) sts of left front. 138 (142: 148: 152: 156: 164) sts.
Work straight until back matches front from marker at shoulder to cast on sts of underarm shaping, ending with a WS row.
Shape underarm
Cast off 10 (10: 10: 11: 11: 12) sts at beg of next 2 rows.
118 (122: 128: 130: 134: 140) sts.
Dec 1 st at each end of next 10 rows, then on 4 foll alt rows, and then on 3 foll 4th rows, ending with a **RS** row.
84 (88: 94: 96: 100: 106) sts.
Work 11 rows, ending with a WS row.
Change to 4mm (US 6) needles.

Next row (RS): K1 (1: 2: 1: 1: 2), (P2, K2) to last 3 (3: 0: 3: 3: 0) sts, P2 (2: 0: 2: 2: 0), K1 (1: 0: 1: 1: 0).
Next row: P1 (1: 0: 1: 1: 0), K2 (2: 0: 2: 2: 0), (P2, K2) to last 1 (1: 2: 1: 1: 2) sts, P1 (1: 2: 1: 1: 2).
These 2 rows form the rib.
Work a further 22 (22: 22: 24: 24: 24) rows in rib, ending with a WS row.
Cast off in rib.

MAKING UP
Pin the knitting out, and press gently as described on the information page.
Join the side and underarm seams using back stitch or mattress st if preferred.
Back neck edging (work both sides the same)
Slip 29 (29: 30: 30: 31: 31) sts from holder at neck onto 4 ½ mm (US 7) needles, rejoin yarn and cont in patt until band fits neatly when slightly stretched across to centre back neck.
Cast off.
With RS facing, join the cast-off ends of the neckband together, then neatly stitch into place around back neck.
Sew on buttons.

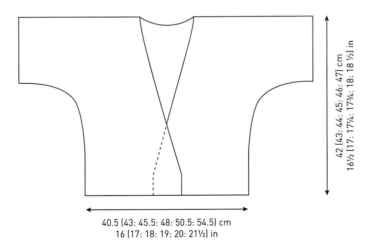

42 (43: 44: 45: 46: 47) cm
16½ (17: 17¼: 17¾: 18: 18 ½) in

40.5 (43: 45.5: 48: 50.5: 54.5) cm
16 (17: 18: 19: 20: 21½) in

Recommendation

Suitable for the knitter with a little experience.
Please see page 22 for photograph.

	XS	S	M	L	XL	XXL	
To fit	81	86	91	97	102	109	cm
bust	32	34	36	38	40	43	in

Rowan Big Wool

| 5 | 5 | 5 | 6 | 6 | 7 | x100gm |

Needles

1 pair 12mm (US 17) needles

Buttons 2

Tension

8 sts and 12 rows to 10 cm measured over
stocking stitch using 12mm (US 17) needles.

STORM

A SLEEVELESS TUNIC FEATURING ZIG-ZAG EYELETS

CARDIGAN (knitted in one piece)

LEFT FRONT

Cast on 21 (22: 23: 25: 26: 27) sts using
12mm (US 17) needles.
Starting with a **WS** row, work lower edging as folls:
Knit 5 rows.
Cont in patt from chart for left front, working
between markers for appropriate size and
setting stitches as folls:
Chart row 1 (RS): P15 (16: 17: 18: 19: 20)
from chart, place a marker on needle before
next st, K6 (6: 6: 7: 7: 7) (for front band).
Chart row 2: K6 (6: 6: 7: 7: 7), slip marker
from left to right needle (on this row and
every foll row), K15 (16: 17: 18: 19: 20)
from chart.
Chart row 3 (RS)(dec): P2tog, patt to marker,
slip marker from left to right needle, K to end.
20 (21: 22: 24: 25: 26) sts.
Keeping front band sts correct, cont in patt
from chart, shaping sides as indicated, until
row 18 is completed, ending with a WS row.
18 (19: 20: 22: 23: 24) sts.
Place a marker at front edge on last row
to indicate position of first button.
Now starting with chart row 3 and repeating
the 16 row patt throughout, cont shaping
side as folls:
Work 4 rows.
Inc 1 st at beg of next row and 2 foll 4th rows,
and then on foll alt row, ending with a **RS** row.
22 (23: 24: 26: 27: 28) sts.
Work 1 row.
Shape front neck slope and underarm
Next row (RS)(inc)(dec): Inc in first st, patt
to 2 sts before marker, P2tog, K to end.
22 (23: 24: 26: 27: 28) sts.
Work 1 row.
Inc 1 st at side edge on next 2 rows, then
turn and cast on 8 (8: 8: 9: 9: 9) sts.
32 (33: 34: 37: 38: 39) sts.
Next row (RS): K8 (8: 8: 9: 9: 9) for armhole
edging, patt to marker, K to end.
Next row: K to marker, patt to last 8 (8: 8: 9:
9: 9) sts, P to end.

Next row (RS)(dec): P8 (8: 8: 9: 9: 9), patt
to 2 sts before marker, P2tog, K to end.
31 (32: 33: 36: 37: 38) sts.
Next row: K to marker, patt to last 8 (8: 8:
9: 9: 9) sts, K to end.
The last four rows form the **horizontal rib**
for armhole edging and are rep along entire
armhole.
Keeping front band, armhole edging and patt on
rem sts correct cont shaping front neck as folls:
Work 4 rows, ending with a WS row.
Dec 1 st as before at front edge on next row,
then on 1 (1: 2: 0: 1: 1) foll 6th row and
then on every foll 4th row to 27 (28: 29:
31: 32: 33) sts, ending with a **RS** row.
Work 5 rows, ending with a WS row.
Place a marker at the armhole edge on
last row to indicate the shoulder line.
Shape back neck
Next row: Work to marker and turn, leaving
rem 6 (6: 6: 7: 7: 7) sts on a holder for back
neck edging. 21 (22: 23: 24: 25: 26) sts.
Work 1 row.
Inc 1 st at neck edge on next row.
Work 1 row.
Inc 1 st at neck edge on next 2 rows, ending
with a WS row. 24 (25: 26: 27: 28: 29) sts.
Work 1 row.
Leave sts on a spare needle.
Mark position of the second button to come
10 rows above first.

RIGHT FRONT

Cast on 21 (22: 23: 25: 26: 27) sts using
12mm (US 17) needles.
Starting with a **WS** row, work lower edging as folls:
Knit 5 rows.
Cont in patt from chart for right front, working
between markers for appropriate size and
setting stitches as folls:
Chart row 1 (RS): K6 (6: 6: 7: 7: 7) (for front
band), place a marker on needle before next
st, P15 (16: 17: 18: 19: 20) from chart.
Chart row 2: K15 (16: 17: 18: 19: 20) from
chart, slip marker from left to right needle (on
this row and every foll row), K6 (6: 6: 7: 7: 7).

Chart row 3 (RS)(dec): Knit to marker, slip marker from left to right needle, patt to last 2 sts, P2tog.

20 (21: 22: 24: 25: 26) sts.

Keeping front band sts correct, cont in patt from chart, shaping sides as indicated, until row 18 is completed, ending with a WS row.

18 (19: 20: 22: 23: 24) sts.

Starting with chart row 3 and repeating the 16 row patt throughout, cont shaping side as folls:

Buttonhole row (RS): K2 (2: 2: 3: 3: 3), K2tog tbl, work to end.

Working a 2nd buttonhole in this way on foll 10th row, cont as folls:

Work 3 rows.

Inc 1 st at end of next row and 2 foll 4th rows, and then on foll alt row, ending with a **RS** row.

22 (23: 24: 26: 27: 28) sts.

Work 1 row.

Complete to match left front, reversing shaping, and ending with a **RS** row.

24 (25: 26: 27: 28: 29) sts.

Join fronts together

Next row (WS): Patt across right front sts, cast on 10 (10: 10: 12: 12: 12) sts, patt across 24 (25: 26: 27: 28: 29) sts of left front. 58 (60: 62: 66: 68: 70) sts.

Work straight until back matches front from marker at shoulder to cast-on sts at end of underarm shaping, ending with a WS row.

Shape underarm

Cast off 8 (8: 8: 9: 9: 9) sts at beg of next 2 rows.

42 (44: 46: 48: 50: 52) sts.

Dec 1 st at each end of next 2 rows, then on 3 foll alt rows, and then on 2 foll 4th rows, ending with a **RS** row.

28 (30: 32: 34: 36: 38) sts.

Work 7 rows, ending with a WS row.

Inc 1 st at each end of next row and 2 foll 6th rows, ending with a **RS** row.

34 (36: 38: 40: 42: 44) sts.

Knit 4 rows, ending with a **RS** row.

Cast off knitwise (on WS).

MAKING UP

Pin the knitting out, and press as described on the information page.

Join the side and underarm seams using back stitch or mattress st if preferred.

Back neck edging (work both sides the same)

Slip 8 (8: 8: 9: 9: 9) from holder at neck onto 12mm (US 17) needles, rejoin yarn

and cont in patt until band fits neatly when slightly stretched across to centre back neck.

Cast off.

With RS facing, join the cast-off ends of the neckband together, then neatly stitch into place around back neck.

Sew on buttons.

KEY

⊡ P on RS, K on WS

⊡⁄ P2tog tbl, yrn

⧵○ yrn, P2tog

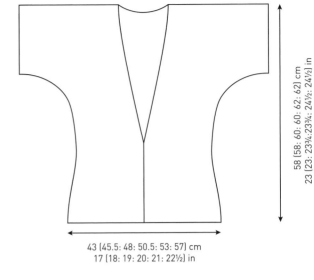

58 [58: 60: 60: 62: 62] cm
23 [23: 23¾:23¾: 24½: 24½] in

43 (45.5: 48: 50.5: 53: 57) cm
17 (18: 19: 20: 21: 22½) in

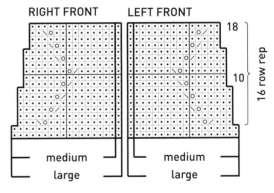

RIGHT FRONT   LEFT FRONT

18

10

16 row rep

x small   x small
small   small

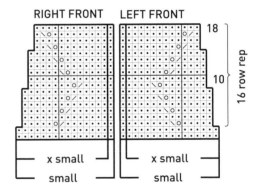

RIGHT FRONT   LEFT FRONT

18

10

16 row rep

medium   medium
large   large

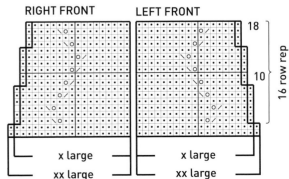

RIGHT FRONT   LEFT FRONT

18

10

16 row rep

x large   x large
xx large   xx large

DUSK

AN UNSTRUCTURED CARDIGAN WITH OPTIONAL KNITTED BELT

Recommendation

Suitable for the novice knitter.

Please see page 23 for photograph.

	XS	S	M	L	XL	XXL	
To fit	81	86	91	97	102	107	cm
bust	32	34	36	38	40	42	in

Rowan Felted Tweed

	7	8	8	8	9	10 x 50gm

Needles

1 pair 3 ¾ mm (no 9) (US 5) needles

Tension

23 sts and 32 rows to 10 cm measured over stocking stitch using 3 ¾ mm (US 5) needles

BACK

Cast on 97 (103: 109: 113: 119: 129) sts using 3 ¾ mm (US 5) needles.

Work 8 (8: 10: 10: 12: 12) rows in garter stitch, i.e. knit every row, ending with a WS row.

Beg with a K row cont in st st until back measures 54.5 (55.5: 56.5: 57.5: 58.5: 59.5) cm, ending with a WS row.

Shape back neck and shoulders

Next row (RS): K until there are 32 (34: 36: 37: 39: 43) sts on right needle and turn, leaving rem sts on a holder.

Work each side of neck separately.

Dec 1 st at beg of next row.

31 (33: 35: 36: 38: 42) sts.

Cast off 10 (10: 11: 11: 12: 13) sts, K to last 2 sts, K2tog. 20 (22: 23: 24: 25: 28) sts.

Next row (WS): P2tog, P to end.

Rep last 2 rows once more.

Cast off rem 8 (10: 10: 11: 11: 13) sts.

With RS facing, rejoin yarn to rem sts, cast off centre 33 (35: 37: 39: 41: 43) sts, K to end.

Complete to match first side rev shaping.

LEFT FRONT

Cast on 76 (80: 85: 88: 94: 100) sts using 3 ¾ mm (US 5) needles.

Row 1 (RS): K to last 16 (17: 18: 19: 19: 20) sts, (P1, K1) 8 (8: 9: 9: 9: 10) times, P0 (1: 0: 1: 1: 0).

Row 2: K0 (1: 0: 1: 1: 0), (P1, K1) 8 (8: 9: 9: 9:10) times, K to end.

Row 3: K to last 16 (17: 18: 19: 19: 20) sts, (K1, P1) 8 (8: 9: 9: 9: 10) times, K0 (1: 0: 1: 1: 0).

Row 4: P0 (1: 0: 1: 1: 0), (K1, P1) 8 (8: 9: 9: 9: 10) times, K to end.

These 4 rows set the stitches, i.e.16 (17: 18: 19: 19: 20) sts in double moss st and rem in garter stitch.

Work 4 (4: 6: 6: 8: 8) more rows, ending with a WS row.

Now working the 16 (17: 18: 19: 19: 20) sts at front edge in double moss st and rem in st st beg with a K row, cont as folls:

Work 4 (4: 2: 2: 2: 2) rows, ending with a WS row.

M, L, XL & XXL sizes only:

Next row (RS)(dec): K to last 20 (21: 21: 22) sts, K2tog tbl, patt to end.

Work 1 row.

Dec 1 st as before at front edge on next row and every foll alt row to 80 (83: 83: 89) sts.

Work 3 rows, ending with a WS row.

All sizes:

Next row (RS)(dec): K to last 18 (19: 20: 21: 21: 22) sts, K2tog tbl, patt to end.

Work 3 rows.

Dec 1 st as before at front edge on next row and every foll 4th row to 56 (60: 63: 66: 66: 72) sts and then on every foll 6th row to 44 (47: 50: 52: 54: 59) sts.

Work straight until front matches back to beg of shoulder shaping, ending with a WS row.

Shape shoulder

Cast off 10 (10: 11: 11: 12: 13) sts at beg of next row and foll alt row.

Work 1 row.

Cast off 8 (10: 10: 11: 11: 13) sts at beg of next row, inc in next st, patt to end.

17 (18: 19: 20: 20: 21) sts.

Keeping patt correct cont for a further 8.5 (9: 10: 10: 10.5: 11) cm.

Cast off.

RIGHT FRONT

Cast on 76 (80: 85: 88: 94: 100) sts using 3 ¾ mm (US 5) needles.

Row 1 (RS): P0 (1: 0: 1: 1: 0), (K1, P1) 8 (8: 9: 9: 9: 10) times, K to end.

Row 2: K to last 16 (17: 18: 19: 19: 20) sts, (K1, P1) 8 (8: 9: 9: 9:10) times, K0 (1: 0: 1: 1: 0).

Row 3: K0 (1: 0: 1: 1: 0), (P1, K1) 8 (8: 9: 9: 9: 10) times, K to end.

Row 4: K to last 16 (17: 18: 19: 19: 20) sts, (P1, K1) 8 (8: 9: 9: 9:10) times, P0 (1: 0: 1: 1: 0).

These 4 rows set the stitches, i.e.16 (17: 18: 19: 19: 20) sts in double moss st and rem in garter stitch.

Work 4 (4: 6: 6: 8: 8) more rows, ending with
a WS row.

Now working the 16 (17: 18: 19: 19: 20) sts
at front edge in double moss st and rem in st
st beg with a K row, cont as folls:

Work 4 (4: 2: 2: 2: 2) rows, ending with
a WS row.

M, L, XL & XXL sizes only:

Next row (RS)(dec): Patt 18 (19: 19: 20) sts,
K2tog, K to end.

Work 1 row.

Dec 1 st as before at front edge on next
row and every foll alt row to 80 (83:
83: 89) sts.

Work 3 rows, ending with a WS row.

All sizes:

Next row (RS)(dec): Patt 16 (17: 18: 19:
19: 20) sts, K2tog, K to end.

Work 3 rows.

Complete as given for left front reversing
shaping.

SLEEVES (both alike)

Cast on 87 (93: 97: 101: 105: 111) sts
using 3 ¾ mm (US 5) needles.

Row 1 (RS): K1, (P1, K1) to end.

Row 2: P1, (K1, P1) to end.

Row 3: Work as row 2.

Row 4: Work as row 1.

These 4 rows form double moss st and are
rep throughout.

Work 20 (20: 22: 22: 24: 24) more rows,
ending with a WS row.

Beg with K row cont in st st until sleeve
measures 35 (36: 37: 38: 39: 40) cm from
cast on edge, ending with a WS row.

Cast off quite loosely.

MAKING UP

Press all pieces as described on information
page.

Join both shoulder seams using back stitch
or mattress st if preferred.

With RS facing, join together the cast-off
edges of neckband, then stitch neatly in
place around back neck.

Place a marker 19.5 (20: 21: 22: 23: 24) cm
down from shoulder seams, on the side edges
of back and fronts.

Place the centre of the cast-off edge of
sleeve to shoulder seam, sew the sleeve
top neatly into place between markers.

Join side and sleeve seams.

OPTIONAL BELT

Cast on 17 (17: 17: 19: 19: 19) sts using
3 ¾ mm (US 5) needles.

Row 1 (RS): P1, (K1, P1) to last 2 sts, K2tog.
16 (16: 16: 18: 18: 18) sts.

Row 2: P1, (K1, P1) to last 3 sts, K1, P into
front and K into back of next st, P1.
17 (17: 17: 19: 19: 19) sts.

Rep these 2 rows until belt measures 148
(152: 156: 160: 164: 168) cm, ending with
a WS row.

Cast off.

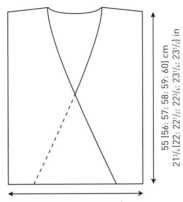

42 (44.5: 47.5: 49: 51.5: 56) cm
16½ (17½: 18¾: 19¼: 20¼: 22) in

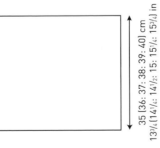

ELIZABETH

SOPHISTICATED JACKET WITH PEPLUM & NOTCHED COLLAR

Recommendation

Suitable for the more experienced knitter.

Please see pages 24 & 25 for photographs.

	XS	S	M	L	XL	XXL	
To fit	**81**	**86**	**91**	**97**	**102**	**109**	**cm**
bust	32	34	36	38	40	43	in

Rowan Summer Tweed

| | 9 | 10 | 11 | 11 | 12 | 13 | x 50gm |

Buttons 3

Needles

1 pair 4mm (no 8) (US 6) needles
1 pair 4 ½ mm (no 7) US 7) needles

Tension

18 sts and 25 rows to 10 cm measured over double moss st using 4 ½ mm (US 7) needles

Double moss st

Row 1 (RS): P1, (K1, P1) to end.
Row 2: K1, (P1, K1) to end.
Row 3: Work as row 2.
Row 4: Work as row 1.

BACK

Cast on 154 (162: 174: 182: 190: 206) sts using 4 ½ mm (US 7) needles.
Row 1 (RS)(dec): (Sl 1, K1, psso) to end.
77 (81: 87: 91: 95: 103) sts.
Shape lower edge
Short row shaping rows 2 & 3 (WS): P to last 22 sts, wrap next st and turn, now cont in **double moss** st as folls: P1, (K1, P1) 16 (18: 21: 23: 25: 29) times (total of 33 (37: 43: 47: 51: 59) sts worked in patt) and 22 sts rem on left needle, wrap next st and turn.
Short row shaping rows 4 & 5: K1, (P1, K1) 20 (22: 25: 27: 29: 33) times and 14 sts rem on left needle, wrap next st and turn, K1, (P1, K1) until 14 sts rem on left needle, wrap next st and turn.
Short row shaping rows 6 & 7: P1, (K1, P1) to last 8 sts, wrap next st and turn, P1, (K1, P1) to last 8 sts, wrap next st and turn.
Short row shaping rows 8 & 9: K1, (P1, K1) to last 4 sts, wrap next st and turn, K1, (P1, K1) to last 4 sts, wrap next st and turn.
Row 10: P1, (K1, P1) to end.
Place a side marker at each end of last row.
Cont in double moss st, working across all sts and shaping sides as folls:
Work 8 rows.
Dec 1 st at each end of next row.
75 (79: 85: 89: 93: 101) sts.
Work 11 rows, ending with a WS row.
Place a marker around the 19th (20th: 22nd: 23rd: 24th: 25th) st in from each end of row.
Next row (RS)(dec): Patt 2tog, patt to 1 st before marker, patt 3tog tbl, patt to next marker, patt 3tog, patt to last 2 sts, patt 2tog.
69 (73: 79: 83: 87: 95) sts.
Work 11 rows.

Next row (RS)(dec): Patt 2tog, patt to 1 st before marker, patt 3tog tbl, patt to next marker, patt 3tog, patt to last 2 sts, patt 2tog.
63 (67: 73: 77: 81: 89) sts.
Work 3 rows.
Change to 4mm (US 6) needles.
Work 12 rows.
Change to 4 ½ mm (US 7) needles.
Work 10 rows.
Next row (RS)(inc): Inc in first st, patt to marked st, M1, patt 1, M1, patt to marked st, M1, patt 1, M1, patt to last st, inc in last st.
69 (73: 79: 83: 87: 95) sts.
Work 11 rows.
Next row (RS)(inc): Inc in first st, patt to marked st, M1, patt 1, M1, patt to marked st, M1, patt 1, M1, patt to last st, inc in last st.
75 (79: 85: 89: 93: 101) sts.
Work 11 rows.
Inc 1 st at each end of next row.
77 (81: 87: 91: 95: 103) sts.
Work straight until back measures 38.5 (38.5: 40: 40: 40: 40)cm from side markers, ending with a WS row.
Shape armholes
Cast off 4 (4: 5: 5: 5: 6) sts at beg of next 2 rows. 69 (73: 77: 81: 85: 91) sts.
Dec 1 st at each end of next 5 (5: 5: 5: 7: 7) rows and 2 (2: 3: 3: 2: 3) foll alt rows, and then on foll 4th row.
53 (57: 59: 63: 65: 69) sts.
Work straight until armhole measures 18 (19: 19: 20: 21: 22)cm, ending with a WS row.
Shape shoulders and back neck
Cast off 5 (5: 5: 6: 6: 6) sts at beg of next 2 rows. 43 (47: 49: 51: 53: 57) sts.
Cast off 5 (5: 5: 5: 5: 6) sts, patt until 8 (9: 9: 9: 9: 9) sts on right needle and turn, leaving rem sts on a holder.
Work each side of neck separately.
Cast off 4 sts, patt to end.
Cast off rem 4 (5: 5: 5: 5: 5) sts.
With RS facing rejoin yarn to rem sts, cast off centre 17 (19: 21: 23: 25: 27) sts, patt to end.
Complete to match first side.

LEFT FRONT

Cast on 92 (96: 102: 106: 110: 118) sts using 4 ½ mm (US 7) needles.

Row 1 (RS)(dec): (Sl 1, K1, psso) to end. 46 (48: 51: 53: 55: 59) sts.

Row 2: Purl.

Shape lower edge and set sts for **double moss st** as folls:

Short row shaping rows 3 & 4: P0 (0: 1: 1: 1: 1), (K1, P1) twice, wrap next st and turn, (K1, P1) to last 0 (0: 1: 1: 1: 1) st, K0 (0: 1: 1: 1: 1).

Short row shaping rows 5 & 6: K0 (0: 1: 1: 1: 1), (P1, K1) 5 times, wrap next st and turn, (P1, K1) to last 0 (0: 1: 1: 1: 1) st, P0 (0: 1: 1: 1: 1).

Short row shaping rows 7 & 8: P0 (0: 1: 1: 1: 1), (K1, P1) to last 28 (30: 33: 35: 37: 41) sts, wrap next st and turn, (K1, P1) to last 0 (0: 1: 1: 1: 1) st, K0 (0: 1: 1: 1: 1).

Short row shaping rows 9 & 10: K0 (0: 1: 1: 1: 1), (P1, K1) to last 18 (20: 23: 25: 27: 31) sts, wrap next st and turn, (P1, K1) to last 0 (0: 1: 1: 1: 1) st, P0 (0: 1: 1: 1: 1).

Short row shaping rows 11 & 12 (dec): Patt 2tog, patt to last 8 (10: 13: 15: 17: 21) sts, wrap next st and turn, patt to end. 45 (47: 50: 52: 54: 58) sts.

Cont in double moss st, working across all sts and shaping side as folls:

Work 10 rows.

Place a marker around the 19th (20th: 22nd: 23rd: 24th: 25th) st in from side edge.

Next row (RS)(dec): Patt 2tog, patt to 1 st before marker, patt 3tog tbl, patt to end. 42 (44: 47: 49: 51: 55) sts.

Work 11 rows.

Next row (RS)(dec): Patt 2tog, patt to 1 st before marker, patt 3tog tbl, patt to end. 39 (41: 44: 46: 48: 52) sts.

Work 3 rows.

Change to 4mm (US 6) needles.

Work 12 rows. Place a **button marker** on the 7th of these 12 rows.

Change to 4 ½ mm (US 7) needles.

Work 10 rows.

Next row (RS)(inc): Inc in first st, patt to marked st, M1, patt 1, M1, patt to end. 42 (44: 47: 49: 51: 55) sts.

Work 11 rows.

Next row (RS)(inc): Inc in first st, patt to marked st, M1, patt 1 and remove marker from this st, M1, patt to last 11 sts, place a marker on needle before next st, P1, place a second marker on needle before next st, patt to end. 45 (47: 50: 52: 54: 58) sts.

Next row (WS): Patt to first marker, slip marker from left to right needle, K1, slip marker from left to right needle, patt to end.

Patt note: From this point (with the RS of work facing you) the sts before the first marker form the left front, the sts after the second marker form the collar and these are divided by 1 st worked in rev st st.

Shape front neck and collar

Cont shaping side edge by inc 1 st as before on the foll 12th row from last inc (as on back) and at the same time shape neck and collar as folls:

Next row (RS)(dec)(inc): Patt to 2 sts before first marker, patt 2tog, P1, inc in next st, patt to end. 45 (47: 50: 52: 54: 58) sts.

Work 1 row.

Next row (RS)(inc): Patt to first marker, P1, inc in next st, patt to end. 46 (48: 51: 53: 55: 59) sts.

Work 1 row.

Rep last 2 rows once more, ending with a WS row. 47 (49: 52: 54: 56: 60) sts.

Next row (RS)(dec)(inc): Patt to 2 sts before first marker, patt 2tog, P1, inc in next st, patt to end. 47 (49: 52: 54: 56: 60) sts.

Work 1 row.

Cont shaping collar and front edge as folls:
Cont shaping collar by **inc** 1 st as before at inside edge of collar on next row and every foll alt row until there are 19 sts to left of marker, then every foll 4th row to 22 (22: 23: 23: 23: 23) sts, and then every foll 6th row to 24 (24: 25: 25: 26: 26) sts, and cont shaping front by **dec** 1 st as before at front edge on every foll 6th row from last dec, and **at the same time** when front matches back to beg of armhole shaping, shape armhole as folls:
Keeping collar and front edge shaping correct, work until front matches back to armhole shaping, ending with a WS row.

Shape armhole

Cast off 4 (4: 5: 5: 5: 6) sts at beg of next row. Work 1 row.

Dec 1 st at armhole edge of next 5 (5: 5: 5: 7: 7) rows and 2 (2: 3: 3: 2: 3) foll alt rows, and then on foll 4th row.

Cont until collar shaping completed, ending with a RS row.

Keeping front dec correct, work a further 10 rows, ending with a RS row.

Work notch in collar

Cast off 10 sts as folls; K1, *wrap yarn around needle and bring loop through, as if knitting a stitch, K1, pass first st over second (1 st cast off; rep from * until 10 sts cast off, then immediately cast on 10 sts as folls: **insert right needle into loop, wrap yarn around needle and bring loop through as if knitting a stitch, wrap the yarn around the right needle and bring loop through, place this last loop on the left needle; rep from ** until 10 sts cast on, work to end.

Keeping front shaping correct, cont until there are 14 (15: 15: 16: 16: 17) sts to right of marker.

Work straight until front match back to shoulder shaping, ending with a WS row.

Shape shoulder

Cast off 5 (5: 5: 6: 6: 6) sts at beg of next row, and 5 (5: 5: 5: 5: 6) sts at beg of foll alt row.

Work 1 row.

Cast off 4 (5: 5: 5: 5: 5) sts, work to end. 25 (25: 26: 26: 27: 27) sts.

Cont in patt for a further 7 (7.5: 8: 8.5: 9: 9.5) cm, ending at **outside edge**.

Next row: Patt to last 8 sts, wrap next st, turn and work to end.

Next row: Patt to last 12 sts, wrap next st, turn and work to end.

Cast off.

Mark position of two more buttons, each to come 12 rows either side of button marker placed earlier.

RIGHT FRONT

Working 3 buttonholes to correspond with positions marked for buttons, complete as given below.

Buttonhole row (RS): Patt 4, patt 2tog tbl, (yon) twice, patt 2tog, patt to end.

Next row: Patt across row working into back of loops made on previous row.

Cast on 92 (96: 102: 106: 110: 118) sts using 4 ½ mm (US 7) needles.

Row 1 (RS)(dec): (Sl 1, K1, psso) to end. 46 (48: 51: 53: 55: 59) sts.

Shape lower edge and set sts for **double moss st** as folls:

Short row shaping rows 2 & 3: P4 (4: 5: 5: 5: 5), wrap next st and turn, (P1, K1) to last 0 (0: 1: 1: 1: 1) st, P0 (0: 1: 1: 1: 1).

Short row shaping rows 4 & 5: K0 (0: 1: 1: 1: 1), (P1, K1) 5 times, wrap next st and turn, (K1, P1) to last 0 (0: 1: 1: 1: 1) st, K0 (0: 1: 1: 1: 1).

Short row shaping rows 6 & 7: P0 (0: 1: 1: 1: 1), (K1, P1) to last 28 (30: 33: 35: 37: 41) sts, wrap next st and turn, (P1, K1) to last 0 (0: 1: 1: 1: 1) st, P0 (0: 1: 1: 1: 1).

Short row shaping rows 8 & 9: K0 (0: 1: 1: 1: 1), (P1, K1) to last 18 (20: 23: 25: 27: 31) sts, wrap next st and turn, (K1, P1) to last 0 (0: 1: 1: 1: 1) st, K0 (0: 1: 1: 1: 1).

Short row shaping rows 10 & 11: P0 (0: 1: 1: 1: 1), (K1, P1) to last 8 (10: 13: 15: 17: 21) sts, wrap next st and turn, patt to last 2 sts, patt 2tog.
45 (47: 50: 52: 54: 58) sts.

Row 12 (WS): Work in patt across all sts.
Cont in double moss st, working across all sts and shaping side as folls:
Work 10 rows.
Place a marker around the 19th (20th: 22nd: 23rd: 24th: 25th) st in from side edge, and with the addition of buttonholes worked to match markers on left front, cont as folls:

Next row (RS)(dec): Patt to 1 st before marker, patt 3tog, patt to last 2 sts, patt 2tog.
42 (44: 47: 49: 51: 55) sts.
Work 11 rows.

Next row (RS)(dec): Patt to 1 st before marker, patt 3tog, patt to last 2 sts, patt 2tog.
39 (41: 44: 46: 48: 52) sts.
Work 3 rows.
Change to 4mm (US 6) needles.
Work 12 rows.
Change to 4 ½ mm (US 7) needles.
Work 10 rows.

Next row (RS)(inc): Patt to marked st, M1, patt 1, M1, patt to last st, inc in last st.
42 (44: 47: 49: 51: 55) sts.
Work 11 rows.

Next row (RS)(inc): Patt 11 sts, place a marker on needle before next st, P1, place a second marker on needle before next st, patt to marked st, M1, patt 1 and remove marker from this st, M1, patt to last st, inc in last st.
45 (47: 50: 52: 54: 58) sts.

Next row (WS): Patt to first marker, slip marker from left to right needle, K1, slip marker from left to right needle, patt to end.

Patt note: From this point (with the RS of work facing you) the sts to the right of the first marker form the collar, and the sts after

the second marker form the right front and these are divided by 1 st worked in **rev** st st. Complete to match left front reversing all shapings.

SLEEVES (work both the same)
Cast on 106 (110: 114: 118: 122: 126) sts using 4 ½ mm (US 7) needles.
Next row (RS)(dec): (Sl 1, K1, psso) to end.
53 (55: 57: 59: 61: 63) sts.
Next row: Purl.
Cont in **double moss st** shaping sides as folls:
Work 2 rows.
Dec 1 st at each end of next row and 3 foll 4th rows, and then on foll 6th row.
43 (45: 47: 49: 51: 53) sts.
Work 15 rows, ending with a WS row.
Inc 1 st at each end of next row.
45 (47: 49: 51: 53: 55) sts.
Work 13 rows.
Inc 1 st at each end of next row and 2 (2: 2: 2: 3: 3) foll 14th rows, and then on 2 (2: 2: 2: 1: 1) foll 12th rows.
55 (57: 59: 61: 63: 65) sts.
Work straight until sleeve measures 44 (45: 46: 47: 48: 49)cm from cast on edge, ending with a WS row.
Shape top
Cast off 4 (4: 5: 5: 5: 6) sts at beg of next 2 rows. 47 (49: 49: 51: 53: 53) sts.
Dec 1 st at each end of next 3 rows and foll alt row. 39 (41: 41: 43: 45: 45) sts.
Work 3 rows, ending with a WS row.
Dec 1 st at each end of next row and every foll 4th row until 31 (31: 31: 33: 33: 33) sts rem.
Work 1 row.
Dec 1 st at each end of next row and 1 (1: 1: 3: 2: 2) foll alt rows, and then on every foll row to 17 (17: 17: 19: 21: 21) sts.
Cast off.

MAKING UP
Press all pieces as described on the information page.
Join both shoulder seams using backstitch or mattress st if preferred.
With RS facing, join cast-off edges of collar together and slip stitch collar into place along back neck.
Join side and sleeve seams.
Set sleeves into armholes.
Sew on buttons to correspond with buttonholes.

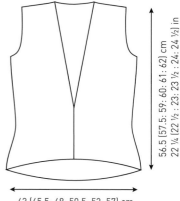

56.5 [57.5: 59: 60: 61: 62] cm
22 ¼ [22 ½ : 23: 23 ½ : 24: 24 ½] in

43 (45.5: 48: 50.5: 53: 57) cm
17 (18: 19: 20: 21: 22½) in

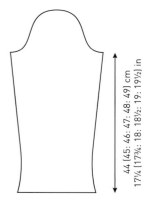

44 (45: 46: 47: 48: 49) cm
17¼ (17¾: 18: 18½: 19: 19½) in

Recommendation

Suitable for the more experienced knitter. Please see page 31 for photograph.

Rowan Bamboo Soft

2 x 50gm

Needles

1 pair 2 ¼ mm (no 13) (US 1) needles
1 pair 3mm (no 11) (US 2/3) needles
1 3.00mm (no 11) (US C2) crochet hook

To fit: Average size

Tension

23 sts and 32 rows to 10 cm measured over pattern (after a light press) using 3mm (US 2/3) needles

BONNIE
SLOUCHY LACE HAT WITH CROCHET OR KNITTED BAND

HAT

Cast on 115 sts using 3mm (US 2/3) needles.

Row 1 (RS): K1, *sl 1, K1, psso, yfwd, K5, K2tog, yfwd, K1; rep from * to last 4 sts, sl 1, K1, psso, yfwd, K2.

Row 2: P1, *P2tog, yrn, P2, yrn, P1, P2tog, P3; rep from * to last 4 sts, P2tog, yrn, P2.

Row 3: K1, *sl 1, K1, psso, yfwd, K3, K2tog, K2, yfwd, K1; rep from * to last 4 sts, sl 1, K1, psso, yfwd, K2.

Row 4: P1, *P2tog, yrn, P2, yrn, P3, P2tog, P1; rep from * to last 4 sts, P2tog, yrn, P2.

Row 5: K1, *sl 1, K1, psso, yfwd, K2, sl 1, K1, psso, K3, yfwd, K1; rep from * to last 4 sts, sl 1, K1, psso, yfwd, K2.

Row 6: P1, *P2tog, yrn, P2, yrn, P3, P2tog tbl, P1; rep from * to last 4 sts, P2tog, yrn, P2.

Row 7: K1, *sl 1, K1, psso, yfwd, K2, yfwd, sl 1, K1, psso, K4; rep from * to last 4 sts, sl 1, K1, psso, yfwd, K2.

Row 8: P1, *P2tog, yrn, P4, P2tog tbl, P1, yrn, P1; rep from * to last 4 sts, P2tog, yrn, P2.

Row 9: K1, *sl 1, K1, psso, (yfwd, K2) twice, sl 1, K1, psso, K2; rep from * to last 4 sts, sl 1, K1, psso, yfwd, K2.

Row 10: P1, *P2tog, yrn, P2, P2tog tbl, P3, yrn, P1; rep from * to last 4 sts, P2tog, yrn, P2.

Row 11: K1, *sl 1, K1, psso, yfwd, K2, yfwd, K3, K2tog, K1; rep from * to last 4 sts, sl 1, K1, psso, yfwd, K2.

Row 12: P1, *P2tog, yrn, P2, P2tog, P3, yrn, P1; rep from * to last 4 sts, P2tog, yrn, P2.

These 12 rows form the pattern.

Rep the 12 row patt 4 times more and then rows 1 – 4 once more, ending with a WS row.

Shape top

Row 1 (RS)(dec): K1, *sl 1, K1, psso, yfwd, K2, P1, K2, P2tog, K1; rep from * to last 4 sts, sl 1, K1, psso, yfwd, K2. 104 sts.

Row 2: P1, *P2tog, yrn, (P2, K1) twice, P1; rep from * to last 4 sts, P2tog, yrn, P2.

Row 3: K1, *sl 1, K1, psso, yfwd, (K2, P1) twice, K1; rep from * to last 4 sts, sl 1, K1, psso, yfwd, K2.

Row 4: Work as row 2.

Row 5 (RS)(dec): K1, *sl 1, K1, psso, yfwd, K2, (P2tog) twice, K1; rep from * to last 4 sts, sl 1, K1, psso, yfwd, K2. 82 sts.

Row 6: P1, *P2tog, yrn, P2, K2, P1; rep from * to last 4 sts, P2tog, yrn, P2.

Row 7: K1, *sl 1, K1, psso, yfwd, K2, P2, K1; rep from * to last 4 sts, sl 1, K1, psso, yfwd, K2.

Row 8: Work as row 6.

Row 9 (RS)(dec): *K2tog tbl, K2tog; rep from * to last 2 sts, K2tog tbl. 41 sts.

Row 10 (dec): P1, *P2tog; rep from * to end. 21 sts.

Row 11 (dec): K1, *K2tog; rep from * to end. 11 sts.

Break yarn and thread through rem 11 sts. Pull up tight and fasten off securely.

Lower edging (crochet)

Join seam, preferably using mattress st. With RS facing, cast on edge uppermost and using 3.00mm (US C2) hook, work crochet edging as folls:

Round 1 (RS): Rejoin yarn to back seam, 1 ch (counts as 1 dc), *1 dc into next st; rep from * to end, ss into first st. 115 sts.

Round 2 (RS)(dec): 1 ch (counts as 1 dc), 1 dc into each of next 3 sts, miss next st, *(1 dc into next st) 4 times, miss next st; rep from * to end, ss into first st. 92 sts.

Round 3 (RS): 1 ch (counts as 1 dc), *1 dc into next st; rep from * to end.

Rep the last round twice more.

Finishing round: Work 1 dc back into last st worked on previous round, *1 dc into next stitch to right; rep from * to end.

Fasten off.

Alternative knitted edging

With RS, cast on edge uppermost and using 2 ¼ mm (US 1) needles, pick up and knit 115 sts along lower edge and work in moss st as folls.

Row 1 (WS): K1, (P1, K1) to end.

Row 2: Work as row 1.

Rep these 2 rows until 10 rows in all completed.

Cast off in moss st (on WS).

Join seam, preferably using mattress st.

EMILY

ELEGANT SWEATER WITH SCOOPED NECK & GATHERED SLEEVES

Recommendation

Suitable for the knitter with a little experience.
Please see pages 26 – 28 for photographs.

	XS	S	M	L	XL	XXL	
To fit	81	86	91	97	102	109	cm
bust	32	34	36	38	40	43	in

Rowan Kid Classic

| | 7 | 7 | 8 | 8 | 9 | 9 | x 50gm |

Needles

1 pair 3 ¾ mm (no 9) (US 5) needles
1 pair 4mm (no 8) (US 6) needles
1 pair 4 ½ mm (no 7) (US 7) needles

Tension

21 sts and 27 rows to 10cm measured over
stocking stitch using 4 ½ mm (US 7) needles

BACK

Cast on 85 (91: 95: 101: 107: 115) sts using
4mm (US 6) needles.
Rows 1 – 6: Knit.
Row 7 & 8: Purl.
Change to 4 ½ mm (US 7) needles.
Rows 9 & 10: Knit.
Rows 11 & 12: Purl.
Row 13: (K2tog, yfwd) to last st, K1.
Row 14: Knit.
Rows 15 & 16: Purl.
Row 17 (RS)(dec): K2, K2tog, K to last 4 sts,
K2tog tbl, K2. 83 (89: 93: 99: 105: 113) sts.
Row 18: Knit.
Rows 19 & 20: Purl.
Rows 21 & 22: Knit.
Rows 23 & 24: Purl.
Row 25: (K2tog, yfwd) to last st, K1.
Row 26: Knit.
Row 27 (RS)(dec): P2, P2tog, P to last 4 sts,
P2tog tbl, P2. 81 (87: 91: 97: 103: 111) sts.
Rows 28 & 29: Purl.
Row 30 (WS): Knit.
Now beg with a K row cont in st st throughout,
and working shapings as folls:
Work 2 (2: 2: 4: 6: 6) rows, ending with a
WS row.
Next row (RS)(dec): K2, K2tog, K to last 4 sts,
K2tog tbl, K2.
79 (85: 89: 95: 101: 109) sts.
Work 5 rows.
Dec 1 st as before at each end of next row
and 2 foll 6th rows.
73 (79: 83: 89: 95: 103) sts.
Work 17 rows, ending with a WS row.
Next row (RS)(inc): K2, M1, K to last 2 sts,
M1, K2.75 (81: 85: 91: 97: 105) sts.
Work 7 rows, ending with a WS row.
Inc 1 st as before at each end of next row
and foll 8th row and then every foll 6th row
to 85 (91: 95: 101: 107: 115) sts.
Work 11 rows, ending with a WS row. (Back
should measure 38 (38: 39: 39: 39: 39)cm.)
Shape armholes
Cast off 4 sts at beg of next 2 rows.
77 (83: 87: 93: 99: 107) sts.

Dec 1 st at each end of next 3 (5: 5: 5: 5: 7)
rows, then on 3 (2: 2: 2: 3: 2) foll alt rows and
then on foll 4th row, ending with a **RS** row.
63 (67: 71: 77: 81: 87) sts.
Work 33 (35: 37: 39: 37: 39) rows straight,
ending with a WS row.
Shape shoulders and back neck
Cast off 6 (6: 7: 7: 8: 8) sts at beg of next
2 rows. 51 (55: 57: 63: 65: 71) sts.
Cast off 6 (6: 6: 7: 7: 8) sts, K until there are
9 (10: 10: 11: 11: 12) sts on right needle and
turn, leaving rem sts on a holder.
Work each side of neck separately.
Cast off 4 sts, work to end.
Cast off rem 5 (6: 6: 7: 7: 8) sts.
With RS facing rejoin yarn and cast off centre
21 (23: 25: 27: 29: 31) sts, K to end.
Complete to match first side, reversing
shaping.

FRONT

Work as given for back until front is 10 rows
shorter then back to beg of armhole shaping,
ending with a WS row.
85 (91: 95: 101: 107: 115) sts.
Shape neck
Next row (RS): K32 (34: 35: 37: 39: 42)
and turn, leaving rem sts on a holder.
Work each side of neck separately.
Dec 1 st at neck edge on next 4 rows and then
on 2 foll alt rows. 26 (28: 29: 31: 33: 36) sts.
Work 1 row, ending with a WS row.
Cont shaping neck and shape armhole as
folls:
Shape armhole
Cast off 4 sts at beg and dec 1 st at end of
row. 21 (23: 24: 26: 28: 31) sts.
Work 1 row.
Dec 1 st at armhole edge on next 3 (5: 5: 5: 5:
7) rows, then on 3 (2: 2: 2: 3: 2) foll alt rows
and then on foll 4th row **and at the same time**
dec 1 st at neck edge on the 4th row from last
dec and then on the foll 4th row, ending with a
RS row. 12 (13: 14: 16: 17: 19) sts.
Work 3 (5: 7: 9: 7: 9) rows straight, ending
with a WS row.

Inc 1 st at neck edge on next row and 3 foll 6th rows and then on foll 8th row, ending with a **RS** row. 17 (18: 19: 21: 22: 24) sts.
Work 3 rows.

Shape shoulder
Cast off 6 (6: 7: 7: 8: 8) sts at beg of next row, and 6 (6: 6: 7: 7: 8) sts at beg of foll alt row.
Work 1 row.
Cast off rem 5 (6: 6: 7: 7: 8) sts.
With RS facing, rejoin yarn to rem sts, cast off centre 21 (23: 25: 27: 29: 31) sts, K to end.
Complete to match first side reversing shaping.

SLEEVES (work both the same)
Cast on 87 (89: 91: 93: 95: 97) sts using 4 ½ mm (US 7) needles.
Beg with a K row cont in st st throughout working shapings as folls:
Work 4 rows, ending with a WS row.
Next row (RS)(dec): K2, K2tog, K to last 4 sts, K2tog tbl, K2. 85 (87: 89: 91: 93: 95) sts.
Work 3 rows.
Dec 1 st as before at each end of next row, then on 2 foll 4th rows, and then on 4 foll 6th rows, ending with a **RS** row.
71 (73: 75: 77: 79: 81) sts.
Work 9 rows.
Dec 1 st as before at each end of next row, then on foll 10th row, and then on foll 18th row. 65 (67: 69: 71: 73: 75) sts.
Work straight until sleeve measures 41 (42: 43: 44: 45: 46) cm, ending with a WS row.

Shape sleeve top
Cast off 4 sts at beg of next 2 rows.
57 (59: 61: 63: 65: 67) sts.
Dec 1 st at each end of next 3 rows, then on foll alt row, and then on every foll 4th row until 41 (41: 43: 45: 45: 47) sts rem.
Work 1 row, ending with a WS row.
Dec 1 st at each end of next row, then on 3 (2: 2: 3: 2: 4) foll alt rows and then on every foll row until 27 (29: 31: 31: 33: 35) sts rem.
Cast off 3 sts at beg of next 2 rows, ending with a WS row.
Cast off rem 21 (23: 25: 25: 27: 29) sts.

Cuff
With RS of sleeve facing, lower edge uppermost and using 3 ¾ mm (US 5) needles, pick up and knit 87 (89: 91: 93: 95: 97) sts across cast on edge.
Next row (WS) (dec): K1, (K2tog) to end.
44 (45: 46: 47: 48: 49) sts.

Rows 1, 2 & 3: Purl.
Row 4: Knit.
Row 5: K1 (0: 1: 0: 1: 0), (K2tog, yfwd) to last st, K1.
Rows 6 & 7: Purl.
Rows 8 & 9: Knit.
Rows 10 & 11: Purl.
Rows 12 & 13: Knit.
Rows 14 & 15: Purl.
Row 16: Knit.
Row 17: Work as row 5.
Rows 18 & 19: Purl.
Rows 20 & 21: Knit.
Rows 22 & 23: Purl.
Cast off knitwise (on WS).

MAKING UP
Press all the pieces as described on the information page.
Join both shoulder seams using back stitch or mattress st if preferred.

Neck edging
Cast on 8 sts using 3 ¾mm (US 5) needles.
Rows 1 & 2: Knit.
Rows 3 & 4: Purl.
Rep the last 4 rows until edging **when slightly stretched** fits around entire neck edge, starting and ending at left shoulder seam.
Pin the edging out on a flat surface, stretching out one edge to form a curve and leaving the other edge completely un-stretched. Lightly steam, making sure the iron does not touch the knitting.
Leave the edging to cool before unpinning and stitching neatly in place.
Join side, sleeve and cuff seams.
Set sleeves into armholes.

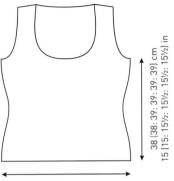

38 [38: 39: 39: 39: 39] cm
15 (15: 15½: 15½: 15½: 15½] in

40.5 [43: 45.5: 48: 50.5: 54.5) cm
16 (17: 18: 19: 20: 21½) in

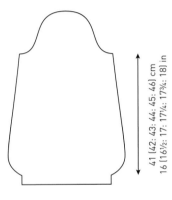

41 [42: 43: 44: 45: 46] cm
16 (16½: 17: 17¼: 17¾: 18] in

TESS

A BOXY CARDIGAN WITH OPEN-WORK PATTERNING

Recommendation

Suitable for the knitter with a little experience.
Please see page 29 for photograph.

	XS–S	M–L	XL–XXL	
To fit	**81–86**	**91–97**	**102–109**	cm
bust	32–34	36–38	40–43	in

Rowan Big Wool

	5	6	7	x 100gm

Needles

1 pair 10mm (no 000) (US 15) needles
1 pair 12mm (US 17) needles

Buttons 2

Tension

8 sts and 12 rows to 10 cm measured over
stocking stitch using 12mm (US 17) needles

FRONTS AND BACK (knitted in one piece)

Cast on 108 (124: 140) sts using 12mm (US
17) needles.
Next row (RS): Sl 1, K1, P to last 2 sts, K1,
P1.
Next row: Sl 1, K1, P to last 2 sts, K1, P1.
Row 1 (RS): Sl 1, K1, *(K2tog) twice, (yfwd)
twice, (sl 1, K1, psso) twice; rep from * to
last 2 sts, K1, P1.
Row 2: Sl 1, K1, *P2tog tbl, (P1, K1) 3 times
into double yfwd, P2tog; rep from * to last
2 sts, K1, P1.
Row 3: Sl 1, K2, *K6 (the 6 new sts above
the yfwd), K2tog but do not slip from needle,
insert right needle between sts just knitted
tog and knit the first st again, then sl both sts
from needle together; rep from *, to last 9 sts,
K8, P1.
Row 4: Sl 1, K1, P to last 2 sts, K1, P1.
Row 5: Sl 1, K5, *(K2tog) twice, (yfwd) twice,
(sl 1, K1, psso) twice; rep from *, to last 6 sts,
K5, P1.
Row 6: Sl 1, K1, P4, *P2tog tbl, (P1, K1)
3 times into double yfwd, P2tog; rep from *
to last 6 sts, P4, K1, P1.
Row 7: Sl 1, K4, *K2tog and K first st again
(as in row 3), K6; rep from * to last 7 sts,
K6, P1.
Row 8: Sl 1, K1, P to last 2 sts, K1, P1.
The last 8 rows form the pattern.
Rep rows 1 – 5 once more, ending with a
RS row.
Next row (WS)(dec): Sl 1, K1, P4, *P2tog tbl,
(P1, K1) **twice** into double yfwd, P2tog; rep
from * to last 6 sts, P4, K1, P1.
84 (96: 108) sts.
XS-S size only
Next row (dec): Sl 1, K1, K2tog, K1, *K2tog
and K first st again (as in row 3), K4; rep from
* to last 5 sts, K1, K2tog tbl, K1, P1. (82 sts)
M-L size only
Next row (dec): Sl 1, K1, K2tog, K1, * (K2tog
and K first st again as in row 3, K4) twice,
(K2tog, K4, K2tog and K first st again, K4)
twice, K2tog and K first st again, K4; rep from
* once more, K3, K2tog tbl, K1, P1. 90 sts.

XL-XXL size only
Next row (dec): Sl 1, K1, K2tog, K1, *K2tog
and K first st again (as in row 3), K1, k2tog,
k1, K2tog and K first st again, K4; rep from
* to last 5 sts, K3, K2tog tbl, K1, P1. 98 sts.
All sizes
Next row (WS): Sl 1, K1, P to last 2 sts,
K1, P1.
82 (90: 98) sts.
Next row (RS): Sl 1, K to last st, P1.
Next row: Sl 1, K1, P to last 2 sts, K1, P1.
Rep the last 2 rows until work measures
27 (28: 29)cm from cast on edge, ending
with a WS row.
Divide for raglans
Keeping 2 sts at front edges correct
throughout cont as folls:
Next row (RS): Sl 1, K until 21 (23: 25) sts on
right needle (these are sts for right front), cast
off next 3 sts, K until there are 34 (38: 42) sts
on right needle for back, cast off next 3 sts,
K to last st, P1 (21 (23: 25) sts), and leaving
stitches for right front and back on holders,
work left front as folls:

LEFT FRONT
Shape raglan
Work 3 rows, ending with a WS row.
Next row (RS)(dec): K2tog, work to end.
Work 1 row.
Dec 1 st as before at raglan edge on next row
and 2 (3: 4) foll alt rows.
17 (18: 19) sts.
Work 1 row.
Next row (RS): Dec 1 st at beg of row, K to
last 11 (12: 13) sts and turn, leaving rem sts
on a holder. 5 sts.
Next row: P2tog tbl, P to end. 4 sts.
Next row: K2tog, K2tog tbl. 2 sts.
Work 1 row.
K2tog and fasten off.

BACK
With **WS** facing rejoin yarn to stitches on
holder for back and work as folls:
Work 3 rows, ending with a WS row.

Next row (RS)(dec): K2tog, K to last 2 sts, K2tog tbl.

Work 1 row.

Dec 1 st at each end of next row and every foll alt row to 20 (22: 24) sts, ending with a **RS** row.

Work 1 row.

Cast off.

RIGHT FRONT

With **WS** facing rejoin yarn to stitches on holder for right front and work as folls:

Keeping front sts correct, work 3 rows.

M-L & XL-XXL sizes only:

Next row (RS): Work to last 2 sts, K2tog tbl.

Work 1 row.

Rep last 2 rows (0: 1) times more.

(22: 23) sts.

All sizes:

Next row (RS)(buttonhole): Sl 1, K1, K2tog tbl, yfwd, K to last 2 sts, K2tog tbl.

Work 1 row.

Dec 1 st as before at raglan edge on next row and 2 foll alt rows, ending with a **RS** row.

17 (18: 19) sts.

Work 1 row.

Next row (RS): K until 11 (12: 13) sts on right needle and leave these sts on a holder, K to last 2 sts, K2tog tbl. 5 sts.

Next row: P3, P2tog. 4 sts.

Next row: K2tog, K2tog tbl. 2 sts.

Work 1 row.

K2tog and fasten off.

SLEEVES (Work both the same)

Cast on 40 (42: 48) sts using 12mm (US 17) needles.

Next row (RS): Purl.

Next row: Purl.

Row 1 (RS): K0 (1: 0), *(K2tog) twice, (yfwd) twice, (sl 1, K1, psso) twice; rep from * to last 0 (1: 0) st, K0 (1: 0).

Row 2: P0 (1: 0), *P2tog tbl, (P1, K1) 3 times into double yfwd, P2tog; rep from * to last 0 (1: 0) st, P0 (1: 0).

Row 3: K1 (2: 1), *K6 (the 6 new sts above the yfwd), K2tog but do not slip from needle, insert right needle between sts just knitted tog and knit the first st again, then sl both sts from needle together; rep from * to last 7 (8: 7) sts, K7 (8: 7).

Row 4: Purl.

Row 5: K4 (5: 4), *(K2tog) twice, (yfwd) twice, (sl 1, K1, psso) twice; rep from *, to last 4 (5: 4) sts, K4 (5: 4).

Row 6: P4 (5: 4), *P2tog tbl, (P1, K1) 3 times into double yfwd, P2tog; rep from * to last 4 (5: 4) sts, P4 (5: 4).

Row 7: K3 (4: 3), *K2tog and K first st again (as in row 3), K6; rep from * to last 5 (6: 5) sts, K2tog and K first st again (as in row 3), K3 (4: 3).

Row 8: Purl.

The last 8 rows form the pattern.

Rep rows 1 – 5 once more, ending with a **RS** row.

Next row (WS)(dec): P2tog, P2 (3: 2), *P2tog tbl, (P1, K1) twice into double yfwd, P2tog; rep from * to last 4 (5: 4) sts, P2 (3: 2) P2tog.

30 (32: 36) sts.

Next row: K3 (4: 3), *K2tog and K first st again (as in row 3), K4; rep from * to last 5 (6: 5) sts, K2tog and K first st again (as in row 3), K3 (4: 3).

Next row (WS): Purl to end dec 1 st at each end of **XL-XXL size only.**

30 (32: 34) sts.

Beg with a K row cont in st st as folls:

Work 6 rows.

Dec 1 st at each end of next row.

28 (30: 32) sts.

Work straight until sleeve measures 27 (28: 29) cm from cast on edge, ending with a WS row.

Shape raglans

Cast off 2 sts at beg of next 2 rows.

24 (26: 28) sts.

Work 2 rows.

Next row (RS)(dec): K2tog, K to last 2 sts, K2tog tbl.

Work 1 row.

Dec 1 as before at each end of next row and every foll alt row to 12 sts, ending with a **RS** row.

Shape sleeve top

Left sleeve

Cast off 5 sts at beg of next row.

Dec 1 st at beg of next row.

Cast off rem 6 sts.

Right sleeve only

Work 1 row.

Cast off 5 sts at beg and dec 1 st at end of next row.

Work 1 row.

Cast off rem 6 sts.

MAKING UP

Press pieces as described on the information page.

Join raglan seams using back stitch or mattess st if preferred.

Neck edging

With RS of right front facing and using 12mm (US 17) needles, slip 11 (12: 13) sts from right front holder onto the right needle, rejoin yarn and pick up and knit 3 sts up right front, 10 sts across top of right sleeve, 20 (21: 25) sts across back, 10 sts across top of left sleeve and 3 sts down left front, and then work across sts on holder as folls: K to last st, P1. 68 (71: 77) sts.

Next row (WS): Sl 1, K1, (P1, K2) to last 3 sts, P1, K1, P1.

Next row: Sl 1, K1, (K1, P2) to last 3 sts, K2, P1.

These 2 rows set the stitches.

Keeping patt correct, work 1 row.

Next row (RS)(buttonhole): Sl 1, K1, K2tog tbl, yon, patt to end.

Work 1 row.

Next row (RS)(dec): Patt 15 (15: 18) sts, (P2tog, K1) 4 times, patt 15 (18: 18) sts, (P2tog, K1) 4 times, patt 14 (14: 17) sts.

Change to 10mm (US 15) needles.

Work 2 rows on sts as set.

Cast off in patt.

Join sleeve seams.

Press seams.

Sew on buttons.

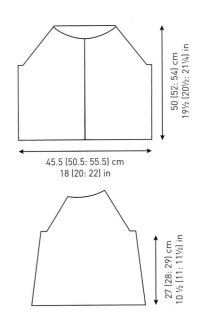

50 [52: 54] cm
19½ (20½: 21¼) in

45.5 (50.5: 55.5) cm
18 (20: 22) in

27 (28: 29) cm
10½ (11: 11½) in

AMORY

AN ELEGANT SWEATER WITH LACE PANELLING

Recommendation

Suitable for the more experienced knitter.
Please see pages 34 & 35 for photographs.

	XS	S	M	L	XL	XXL	
To fit	81	86	91	97	102	109	cm
bust	32	34	36	38	40	43	in

Rowan Bamboo Soft

	10	11	12	13	14	14	x 50gm

Buttons 10

Needles

1 pair 3mm (no 11) (US 2/3) needles
1 pair 3¼mm (no 10) (US 3) needles
1 pair 3 ¾mm (no 9) (US 5) needles
3.50mm (no 9) (US E4) crochet hook

Tension

24 sts and 30 rows to 10cm measured over
reversed stocking stitch using 3 ¾mm (US 5)
needles and after steaming

Tension note:

The Bamboo Soft yarn relaxes after steaming.
This opens the knitting and changes the
tension by approximately one stitch in
the width. Therefore your knitting, before
steaming, should have a tension of 24 sts
and 30 rows to 10 cm.

Lace panel (worked over 7 sts)
Row 1 (RS): K2tog, (yfwd, K1) 3 times, yfwd,
K2tog tbl. 9 sts.
Row 2: Purl.
Row 3: K2tog, K5, K2tog tbl. 7 sts.
Row 4: Purl.

BACK

Lower edging

Cast on 18 (18: 18: 20: 20: 20) sts using
3 ¼ mm (US 3) needles.
**Row 1 (RS): K to last 5 sts, yfwd, K2tog, K3.
Row 2: Sl 1, K4, yfwd, K2tog, K to end.
Rows 3 & 4: Work as rows 1 & 2.
Rows 5: K to last 5 sts, yfwd, K2tog, inc
(by knitting into front and back) in each
of next 3 sts.
Rows 6: Cast off 3 sts, K until 5 sts on right
needle, yfwd, K2tog, K to end. **
Rep the last 6 rows 29 (31: 33: 35: 37: 39)
times in all and then work rows 1 – 4 again.
Cast off and break yarn.

Upper back

With RS of lower edging facing and using
3 ¾ mm (US 5) needles, pick up and knit
89 (95: 101: 107: 113: 121) sts along the
top (long straight edge) of lower edging.
Cont in rev st st placing lace panels as folls:
Shape lower edge as folls:
Next row (WS): K28 (31: 33: 36: 38: 42),
*P7, K6 (6: 7: 7: 8: 8); rep from * once more,
P7, K28 (31: 33: 36: 38: 42).
Short row shaping rows 1 & 2: P28 (31: 33:
36: 38: 42), *work row 1 of lace panel,
P6 (6: 7: 7: 8: 8); rep from * once more,
work row 1 of lace panel, P0 (2: 4: 7: 9: 13),
wrap next st and turn, K0 (2: 4: 7: 9: 13),
*work row 2 of lace panel, K6 (6: 7: 7: 8: 8);
rep from * once more, work row 2 of lace
panel, K0 (2: 4: 7: 9: 13), wrap next st
and turn.
These last 2 rows set the sts for the lace
panels with rem sts worked in rev st st.
Place a marker at each end of last row.
Keeping lace panels correct, cont shaping
lower edge as folls:

Short row shaping rows 3 & 4: *Work to last
22 (23: 23: 23: 23: 23) sts, wrap next st and
turn; rep from * once more.
Short row shaping rows 5 & 6: *Work to last
18 sts, wrap next st and turn; rep from * once
more.
Short row shaping rows 7 & 8: *Work to last
15 sts, wrap next st and turn; rep from * once
more.
Short row shaping rows 9 & 10: *Work to last
12 sts, wrap next st and turn; rep from *once
more.
Short row shaping rows 11 & 12: *Work to
last 9 sts, wrap next st and turn; rep from *
once more.
Short row shaping rows 13 & 14: *Work to
last 6 sts, wrap next st and turn; rep from *
once more.
Short row shaping rows 15 & 16: *Work to
last 3 sts, wrap next to and turn; rep from *
once more.
Row 17 (RS): Patt to end.
Row 18: Work in patt across all sts.
Cont on sts as set shaping sides as folls:
Work 2 rows.
Next row (RS)(dec): P2, P2tog, patt to last
4 sts, P2tog tbl, P2.
87 (93: 99: 105: 111: 119) sts.
Work 3 rows.
Dec 1 st as before at each end of next row
and 2 foll 4th rows.
81 (87: 93: 99: 105: 113) sts.
Work 13 rows, ending with a WS row.
Next row (RS)(inc): P2, M1, patt to last 2 sts,
M1, P2.
83 (89: 95: 101: 107: 115) sts.
Work 7 rows.
Inc 1 st as before at each end of next row
and 4 foll 8th rows.
93 (99: 105: 111: 117: 125) sts.
Work straight until back measures 28 (28:
28.5: 28.5: 29: 29)cm from marked row,
ending with a WS row.
Shape armholes
Cast off 4 sts at beg of next 2 rows.
85 (91: 97: 103: 109: 117) sts.

Dec 1 st at each end of next 5 (5: 5: 7: 7: 9) rows, then on 2 (3: 4: 3: 4: 4) foll alt rows, and then on foll 4th row.
69 (73: 77: 81: 85: 89) sts.
Work straight until armhole measures 18 (19: 19.5: 20: 21: 22)cm, ending with a WS row.

Shape shoulders and back neck
Cast off 6 (6: 6: 7: 7: 7) sts at beg of next 2 rows. 57 (61: 65: 67: 71: 75) sts.
Cast off 5 (6: 6: 6: 7: 7) sts, work until there are 9 (9: 10: 10: 10: 11) sts on right needle and turn, leaving rem sts on a holder.
Work each side of neck separately.
Cast off 4 sts, work to end.
Cast off rem 5 (5: 6: 6: 6: 7) sts.
With RS facing rejoin yarn to rem sts, cast off centre 29 (31: 33: 35: 37: 39) sts, work to end.
Complete to match first side, reversing shapings.

FRONT
Work as given for back to shape armholes, ending with a WS row.

XS, S & M sizes only
Shape armholes and front neck
Next row (RS): Cast off 4 sts, patt until 35 (37: 39) sts on right needle and turn, leaving rem sts on a holder.
Work each side of neck separately.
Dec 1 st at beg of next row. 34 (36: 38) sts.

L, XL & XXL sizes only
Shape armholes and front neck
Cast off 4 sts at beg of next 2 rows.
Dec 1 st at each end of next (2: 2: 4) rows. (99: 105: 109) sts.
Next row (RS): Dec 1 st, patt until (39: 41: 42) sts on right needle and turn, leaving rem sts on a holder.
Work each side of neck separately.
Dec 1 st at each end of next row. (37: 39: 40) sts.

All sizes
Dec 1 st at armhole edge on the next 5 (5: 5: 3: 3: 3) rows, then on 2 (3: 4: 3: 4: 4) foll alt rows, and then on foll 4th row (as given for back), and **at the same time** shape neck as folls:
Dec 1 st at neck edge on the next 3 rows, 4 (4: 4: 5: 5: 5) foll alt rows, and then on foll 4th row.
Work 7 rows.
18 (19: 20: 21: 22: 23) sts.

Dec 1 st at neck edge on next row and foll 16th row. 16 (17: 18: 19: 20: 21) sts.
Work straight until front matches back to start of shoulder shaping, ending with a WS row.

Shape shoulder
Cast off 6 (6: 6: 7: 7: 7) sts at beg of next and 5 (6: 6: 6: 7: 7) sts, at beg of foll alt row.
Work 1 row.
Cast off rem 5 (5: 6: 6: 6: 7) sts.
With RS facing rejoin yarn to rem sts, cast off centre 15 (17: 19: 19: 21: 23) sts, work to end.
Complete to match first side reversing shaping.

Sleeves (work both the same)
Work lower edging as folls:
Cast on 18 (18: 18: 20: 20: 20) sts using 3 ¼ mm (US 3) needles.
Work as given for back from ** to **.
Rep the last 6 rows 14 (14: 15: 15: 16: 17) times in all and then work rows 1 – 4 again.
Cast off and break yarn.

Upper sleeve
With RS of lower edging facing and using 3 ¾ mm (US 5) needles, pick up and knit 50 (52: 54: 56: 58: 60) sts along the top (long straight edge) of lower edging.
Next row (WS): Knit to end.
Cont in rev st st, shaping sides as folls:
Next row (RS)(inc): P2, M1p, P to last 2 sts, M1p, P2. 52 (54: 56: 58: 60: 62) sts.
Work 11 rows, ending with a WS row.
Inc 1 st as before at each end of next row and 2 (4: 4: 4: 4: 4) foll 12th rows, and then on every foll 10th row to 70 (72: 74: 76: 78: 80) sts.
Work straight until sleeve measures 44 (45: 46: 47: 48: 49)cm (including edging), ending with a WS row.

Shape top
Cast off 4 sts at beg of next 2 rows.
62 (64: 66: 68: 70: 72) sts.
Dec 1 st at each end of next 3 rows, then on foll alt row, and then on every foll 4th row to 46 (48: 48: 50: 50: 52) sts.
Work 1 row, ending with a WS row.
Dec 1 st at each end of next row and 4 (4: 4: 5: 4: 5) foll alt rows and then on every row to 26 (28: 28: 28: 30: 30) sts, ending with a WS row.
Cast off 3 sts at beg of next 2 rows.
Cast off rem 20 (22: 22: 22: 24: 24) sts.

MAKING UP
Pin the pieces out, and **steam** gently without allowing the iron to touch the yarn.
Join right shoulder seam using back stitch or mattress st if preferred.

Neck edging
With RS facing and using 3 mm (US 2/3) needles, pick up and knit 42 (44: 46: 46: 46: 48) sts down left front neck, 15 (17: 19: 19: 21: 23) across centre front, 42 (44: 46: 46: 46: 48) up left front neck and 37 (39: 41: 43: 45: 47) sts across back.
136 (144: 152: 154: 158: 166) sts.
Knit 8 (8: 8: 10: 10: 10) rows.
Cast off knitwise (on WS).
Join left shoulder and neck edging seam.
Join side and sleeve seams, leaving side seams open at border edges.
Set sleeves into armholes.
Using 3.50mm (US E4) crochet hook, make 5 button loops along each side of front border edge.
Sew on buttons to correspond with button loops.

40.5 (43: 45.5: 48: 50: 54.5) cm
16 (17: 18: 19: 20: 21½) in

46 (47: 48: 48.5: 50: 51] cm
18 (18½: 19: 19¼: 19¾: 20] in

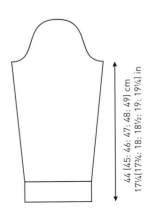

44 (45: 46: 47: 48: 49] cm
17¾(17¾: 18: 18½: 19: 19¼] in

FLOURISH

FLOUNCY & FROTHY, A CROCHET SCARF WITH BEADED DETAIL

Recommendation
Suitable for average ability.
Please see pages 32 & 33 for photographs.

Size
One size

Rowan Kidsilk Haze
4 x 25gm

Beads
Approximately 1,000

Crochet hook
9.00 mm (US13-15) crochet hook

Finished length
Approximately 175cm (69 in) long

CENTRE CHAIN
Using 9.00 mm (US13-15) hook and yarn
double, make 122 ch – make sure the chain
is not tight. It should measure approximately
165cm long.
Important note: The centre chain is the
foundation of the scarf, and each chain is
increased several times over the three row
patt. If you need to work extra chains to
achieve the required length, you will have
insufficient yarn and beads to complete the
scarf, therefore it is very important that your
tension for the centre chain is correct.

FIRST SIDE
Row 1 (RS): 1 htr into 3rd chain from hook,
2 htr into all rem ch, turn. 240 sts.
Row 2: 3ch (counts as tr), 1 tr into first st,
2 tr into each st to end, turn. 480 sts.
Row 3: 4ch (counts as dtr) 1 dtr into each
st to end, turn.
Break yarn.
Thread approximately 100-150 beads onto
one strand of yarn (don't be tempted to put
too many on at once because this would make
the yarn too heavy to work with) and rejoin
just this one strand of yarn to work and cont
as folls:
Row 4: *Work 1 dc into next stitch, bring 1
bead to about 2 cm from hook, work 1 dc into
same stitch; rep from * to end, breaking yarn
and threading beads on as required.
Work ss across the ends of the rows to the
centre chain and work second side as folls:

SECOND SIDE
Row 1 (RS): 2ch (counts as 1 htr), 1 htr into
first ch, 2 htr into all rem sts, turn. 240 sts.
Complete as for first side.
Fasten off.

Recommendation

Suitable for the novice knitter.
Please see page 36 for photograph.

	XS	S	M	L	XL	XXL	
To fit	81	86	91	97	101	106/112	cm
bust	32	34	36	38	40	42/44	ins

Rowan Biggy Print

| | 3 | 3 | 4 | 4 | 4 | 5 | x 100gm |

Needles

1 pair 20mm (US 36) needles
1 pair 15mm (US 19) needles

Tension

5 ½ sts and 7 rows to 10cm measured over
reversed stocking stitch using 20mm (US 36)
needles.

BLESS

A SIMPLE SHRUG WORKED IN AN OVERSIZED YARN

Special abbreviation

MP = Make picot: cast on 1 st, cast off 1 st.

SHRUG

Cast on 14 (15: 15: 16: 16: 17) sts using
20 mm (US 36) needles.
Beg with a P row, work 4 rows in rev st st.
Inc 1 st at each end of next row and foll
4th row. 18 (19: 19: 20: 20: 21) sts.
Knit 1 row, ending with a WS row.
Place a marker at each end of last row.
Next row (RS): MP, K1, P to last 2 sts, K2.
Next row: MP, K to end.
These 2 rows set the stitches.
Work a further 18 (20: 22: 24: 26: 28) rows
as set.
Place a marker at each end of last row.
Working in rev st st across all sts,
cont as folls:
Dec 1 st at each end of next row and foll
4th row. 14 (15: 15: 16: 16: 17) sts.
Work 3 rows.
Cast off.

CUFF (both alike)

Cast on 4 (4: 4: 5: 5: 5) sts using 15 mm
(US 19) needles.
Knit 2 rows.
Next row (RS): MP, K to end.
Next row: Knit.
Rep these 2 rows 11 (12: 12: 13: 13: 13)
times more (26 (28: 28: 30: 30: 30) rows
completed).
Cast off.

MAKING UP

Press main piece as described on the
information page.
Stitch the straight edge of the cuff neatly
into place along the short edges.
Join the underarm seam from picot edge
to markers, try the shrug on and adjust the
length of the seams so that the shrug fits
closely across the lower back.

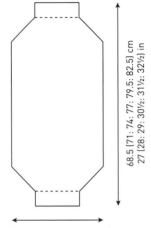

68.5 (71: 74: 77: 79.5: 82.5) cm
27 (28: 29: 30½: 31½: 32½) in

32.5 (24.5: 34.5: 36.5: 36.5: 38) cm
13 (13½: 13½: 14½: 14½: 15) in

VALIANT
TEXTURED SWEATER WITH CABLE DETAIL TO THE NECKLINE

Recommendation
Suitable for the knitter with a little experience.
Please see page 38 for photograph.

	XS	S	M	L	XL	XXL	
To fit	**81**	**86**	**91**	**97**	**101**	**109**	cm
bust	32	34	36	38	40	43	ins

Rowan Cocoon
	8	8	9	9	10	11	x100gm

Needles
1 pair 7mm (no 2) (US 10 ½) needles
1 pair 8mm (no 0) (US 11) needles
Cable needle

Tension
14 sts and 17 rows to 10cm measured over
textured pattern using 8mm (US 11) needles

Special abbreviations:
MP = Make picot: Cast on 1 st, cast off 1 st.
Make bobble: K into front, back, front and
back of next st, turn, K4, turn, (K2tog) twice,
pass first st over second.
C8B = Slip next 4 sts onto a cable needle
and hold at back, K4, K4 from cable needle.
C8F = Slip next 4 sts onto a cable needle
and hold at front, K4, K4 from cable needle.

BACK
Cast on 63 (67: 71: 73: 77: 83) sts using
8mm (US 11) needles and work in patt as folls:
Row 1 (RS): K1, (P1, K1) to end.
Row 2: Knit.
These 2 rows form the patt and are rep
throughout.
Work 10 more rows, ending with a WS row.
Dec 1 st at each end of next row and 2 foll
6th rows, and then on 2 foll 4th rows.
53 (57: 61: 63: 67: 73) sts.
Work 15 rows, ending with a WS row.
Inc 1 st at each end of next row and 2 foll
8th rows.
59 (63: 67: 69: 73: 79) sts.
Work straight until back measures 41 (41: 42:
42: 42: 42)cm from cast on edge, ending with
a WS row.
Shape raglans
Cast off 4 (4: 5: 5: 5: 6) sts at beg of next
2 rows. 51 (55: 57: 59: 63: 67) sts.
Next row (RS)(dec): P1, P2tog tbl, patt to
last 3 sts, P2tog, P1.
Next row: Knit. **
Dec 1 st as before at each end of next row
and every foll alt row until 21 (23: 25: 25:
27: 29) sts rem, ending with a **RS** row.
Work 1 row.
Cast off.

FRONT
Work as given for back to **.
Dec 1 st as before at each end of next row
and every foll alt row until 29 (31: 35: 35:
39: 41) sts rem, ending with a **RS** row.
Work 1 row.

Shape front neck
Next row (RS)(dec): P1, P2tog tbl, patt until
7 (7: 9: 9: 11: 11) sts on right needle and
turn, leaving rem sts on a holder.
Work each side of neck separately.
Keeping raglan shaping correct, dec 1 st at
raglan armhole edge of 2nd and foll 0 (0: 1:
1: 2: 2) alt rows and **at the same time** dec
1 st at neck edge of next 3 (3: 4: 4: 4: 4)
rows, then on foll 0 (0: 0: 0: 1: 1) alt row.
3 sts.
Work 0 (0: 1: 1: 1: 1) row, ending with a WS row.
P3tog and fasten off.
With RS facing, rejoin yarn to rem sts, cast off
centre 13 (15: 15: 15: 15: 17) sts, patt to last
3 sts, P2tog, P1.
Complete to match first side, reversing
shaping.

SLEEVES (both alike)
Cast on 51 (53: 55: 57: 59: 61) sts using
8mm (US 11) needles and work in patt as folls:
Row 1 (RS): K1, (P1, K1) to end.
Row 2: Knit.
These 2 rows form the patt and are rep
throughout.
Work 12 more rows, ending with a WS row.
Dec 1 st at each end of next row and 2 foll
10th rows, and then on foll 16th row.
43 (45: 47: 49: 51: 53) sts.
Work straight until sleeve measures 44 (44:
46: 46: 48: 48)cm, ending with a WS row.
Shape raglans
Cast off 4 (4: 5: 5: 5: 6) sts at beg of next
2 rows. 35 (37: 37: 39: 41: 41) sts.
Next row (RS): P2, patt to last 2 sts, P2.
Next row: Knit.
Next row (RS)(dec): P1, P2tog tbl, patt to
last 3 sts, P2tog, P1.
Next row: Knit.
Work 0 (0: 0: 2: 2: 2) rows.
Dec 1 st as before at each end of next row,
and **for XXL size only** 2 foll 4th rows, and
then for all sizes dec 1 st as on every foll alt
row until 7 (9: 9: 11: 11: 13) sts rem, ending
with a **RS** row.

Shape sleeve top
Left sleeve only
Cast off 3 (4: 4: 5: 5: 6) sts at beg of
next row.
Dec 1 st as before at beg of next row.
Cast off rem 3 (4: 4: 5: 5: 6) sts.
Right sleeve only
Work 1 row.
Cast off 3 (4: 4: 5: 5: 6) sts at beg and dec
1 st at end of next row. Work 1 row.
Cast off rem 3 (4: 4: 5: 5: 6) sts.

MAKING UP
Press all pieces as described on the
information page.
Join raglan seams using back stitch or
mattress stitch if preferred.
Collar
Cast on 48 (48: 50: 50: 52: 52) sts using
7mm (US 10 ½) needles.
Row 1 (RS): K25 (25: 27: 27: 29: 29), P3,
K12, P3, K5.
Row 2: MP, K until 8 sts on right needle,
P12, K3, P to end.
Row 3: P25 (25: 27: 27: 29: 29), P1, make
bobble, P1, C8B, K4, P1, make bobble, P1, K5.
Row 4: MP, K until 8 sts on right needle,
P12, K3, K to end.
Row 5: Work as row 1.
Row 6: Work as row 2.
Row 7: P25 (25: 27: 27: 29: 29), P1, make
bobble, P1, K4, C8F, P1, make bobble, P1, K5.
Row 8: Work as row 4.
These 8 rows form the patt and are rep
throughout.
Cont in patt until 14 (16: 18: 19: 20: 22) patt
repeats in total have been completed, ending
with patt row 8.
Cast off.
Matching the pattern, carefully stitch the cast-
off and cast-on edges together to form a tube.
With WS of collar and RS of sweater facing,
and placing seam of collar to centre back
neck, pin the collar evenly into place around
the neck edge. Stitch into place.
Join side and sleeve seams.
Press seams.

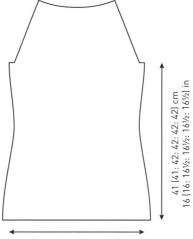

41 (41: 42: 42: 42: 42) cm
16 (16: 16½: 16½: 16½: 16½) in

43 (45.5: 48: 50.5: 53: 57) cm
17 (18: 19: 20: 21: 22½) in

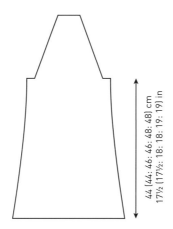

44 (44: 46: 46: 48: 48) cm
17½ (17½: 18: 18: 19: 19) in

Recommendation

Suitable for the knitter with a little experience.
Please see pages 40 & 41 for photographs.

	XS	S	M	L	XL	XXL	
To fit	**81**	**86**	**91**	**97**	**102**	**109**	cm
bust	32	34	36	38	40	43	in

Rowan Bamboo Soft

	10	11	12	13	14	14	x 50gm

Needles

1 pair 3mm (no 11) (US 2/3) needles
1 pair 3 ¼mm (no 10) (US 3) needles
1 pair 3 ¾mm (no 9) (US 5) needles

Buttons 8

Tension

24 sts and 30 rows to 10cm measured over
reversed stocking stitch using 3 ¾mm (US 5)
needles

Tension note:

The Bamboo Soft yarn relaxes after steaming.
This opens the knitting and changes the
tension by approximately one stitch in
the width. Therefore your knitting, before
steaming, should have a tension of 24 sts and
30 rows to 10 cm.

FAITH

PRETTY BLOUSE WITH A PEPLUM & LACE PANELLING

BACK

Lower edging

Cast on 23 (23: 23: 25: 25: 25) sts using
3 ¼ mm (US 3) needles.

**Shape side

Next row (RS): K to last 5 sts, yfwd,
K2tog, K3.

Short row shaping: Sl 1, K4, yfwd, K2tog,
K until 9 sts on right needle, wrap next stitch
and turn, K to last 5 sts, yfwd,
K2tog, K3.

Short row shaping: Sl 1, K4, yfwd, K2tog, K
until 15 sts on right needle, wrap next stitch
and turn, K to last 5 sts, yfwd, K2tog, K3.

Short row shaping: Sl 1, K4, yfwd, K2tog,
K until 21 sts on right needle, wrap next
stitch and turn, K to last 5 sts, yfwd, K2tog,
inc (by knitting into front and back) in each
of next 3 sts.

26 (26: 26: 28: 28: 28) sts.

Next row (WS): Cast off 3 sts, K until 5 sts
on right needle, yfwd, K2tog, K to end.
23 (23: 23: 25: 25: 25) sts.
This completes the side shaping.

Row 1 (RS): K to last 5 sts, yfwd, K2tog, K3.
Row 2: Sl 1, K4, yfwd, K2tog, K to end.
Rows 3 & 4: Work as rows 1 & 2.
Rows 5: K to last 5 sts, yfwd, K2tog, inc in
each of next 3 sts.
Rows 6: Cast off 3 sts, K until 5 sts on right
needle, yfwd, K2tog, K to end. **
Rep the last 6 rows 26 (28: 30: 31: 33: 36)
times in all.

Shape side

***Short row shaping:** Sl 1, K4, yfwd, K2tog,
K until 21 sts on right needle, wrap next
stitch and turn, K to last 5 sts, yfwd, K2tog,
K3 sts.

Short row shaping: Sl 1, K4, yfwd, K2tog, K
until 15 sts on right needle, wrap next stitch
and turn, K to last 5 sts, yfwd, K2tog, K3.

Short row shaping: Sl 1, K4, yfwd, K2tog,
K until 9 sts on right needle, wrap next stitch
and turn, K to last 5 sts, yfwd, K2tog, K3.
Work 1 row.
Cast off and break yarn. ***

Upper back

With RS of lower edging facing and using
3 ¾ mm (US 5) needles, pick up and knit
77 (85: 89: 93: 99: 109) sts along the top
(long straight edge) of lower edging, turn
and **knit** to end.

Cont in **rev st st** and shaping sides as folls:
Beg with a P row, work 2 (2: 4: 4: 4: 4) rows.
Next row (RS)(inc): P2, M1p, P to last 2 sts,
M1p, P2.
79 (87: 91: 95: 101: 111) sts.
Work 5 rows.
Inc 1 st as before at each end of next row and
foll 6th row. 83 (91: 95: 99: 105: 115) sts.
Work 5 rows, ending with a WS row.
Cont from chart for back, setting sts for eyelet
panel as folls:
Chart row 1 (RS)(inc): P2, M1p, P until
35 (39: 41: 43: 46: 51) sts on right needle,
P2tog tbl, yrn, P5, yrn, P2tog, P to last 2 sts,
M1p, P2.
85 (93: 97: 101: 107: 117) sts.
Chart row 2: Knit.
Keeping side shaping correct cont until
chart row 16 (16: 16: 18: 18: 18) has been
completed ending with a WS row.
Patt note: The 3 smaller sizes have a panel
of 8 ridges, whilst the 3 largest sizes have
a panel of 10 ridges.
Working eyelet patt as set throughout, cont
shaping sides as before on every foll 6th row
to until to 97 (103: 109: 113: 119: 129) sts.
Work straight until back measures 21 (21:
21.5: 22: 22: 22) cm from top of edging,
ending with a WS row.
Shape armholes
Cast off 4 (4: 4: 5: 5: 5) sts at beg of next
2 rows. 89 (95: 101: 103: 109: 119) sts.
Dec 1 st at each end of next 5 (7: 7: 7: 7: 11)
rows, and 4 (3: 4: 4: 5: 4) foll alt rows, and then
on foll 4th row. 69 (73: 77: 79: 83: 87) sts.
Work straight until armhole measures 18 (19:
19.5: 20: 21: 22)cm, ending with a WS row.
Shape shoulders and back neck
Cast off 6 (6: 7: 7: 7: 7) sts at beg of next 2 rows.
57 (61: 63: 65: 69: 73) sts.

Cast off 6 (6: 6: 6: 7: 7) sts, work until 9 (10: 10: 10: 10: 11) sts on right needle and turn, leaving rem sts on a holder.
Work each side of neck separately.
Cast off 4 sts at beg of next row.
Cast off rem 5 (6: 6: 6: 6: 7) sts.
With RS facing rejoin yarn to rem sts, cast off centre 27 (29: 31: 33: 35: 37) sts, work to end.
Complete to match first side rev shaping.

LEFT FRONT
Lower edging
Cast on 23 (23: 23: 25: 25: 25) sts using 3 ¼ mm (US 3) needles.
Work as given for the back from ** to **, placing a marker at **beg** of last row.
Rep the last 6 rows 8 (9: 10: 11: 12: 13) and then rows 1 to 4 again, ending with a WS row.
Shape front curve
Row 1 (RS) (dec): K to last 8 sts, K2tog, K1, yfwd, K2tog, inc in each of next 3 sts.
Work 3 rows in patt. 22 (22: 22: 24: 24: 24) sts.
Row 5 (RS) (dec): K to last 8 sts, K2tog, K1, yfwd, K2tog, K3. 21 (21: 21: 23: 23: 23) sts.
Work 3 rows in patt.
Row 9 (RS) (dec): Work as row 5.
20 (20: 20: 22: 22: 22) sts.
Work 3 rows in patt.
Keeping patt correct, dec 1 st as before on next row and every foll alt row until 9 sts rem, ending with a **RS** row.
Next row (WS): (dec): Patt to last 2 sts, K2tog. 8 sts.
Keeping patt correct as far as possible and then working in garter st, cont dec 1 st at beg of next row and at the **same edge** on every foll row until 1 st remains.
Fasten off and break yarn.

Upper left front
With RS of lower edging facing and using 3 ¾ mm (US 5) needles, starting at **cast on** edge, pick up and knit 47 (50: 53: 55: 58: 63) sts across long straight edge, to 'fasten off' point, turn and **knit** to end.
Cont in **rev st st**, setting stitch for front band and shaping sides as folls:
Next row (RS): P to last 6 sts, K6 to form the button band.
Next row: Knit.
Working 6 sts at centre front in garter st throughout cont as folls:
Work 0 (0: 2: 2: 2: 2) rows.
Next row (RS)(inc): P2, M1p, P to last 6 sts, K6. 48 (51: 54: 56: 59: 64) sts.
Work 5 rows.
Inc 1 st as before at beg of next row and foll 6th row. 50 (53: 56: 58: 61: 66) sts.
Work 5 rows, ending with a WS row.
Cont from chart for left front, setting stitches for eyelet panel as folls:
Chart row 1 (RS)(inc): P2, M1p, P until 35 (39: 41: 43: 46: 51) sts on right needle, P2tog tbl, yrn, P5, K6.
51 (54: 57: 59: 62: 67) sts.
Chart row 2: Knit.
Keeping side shaping correct cont until chart row 16 (16: 16: 18: 18: 18) has been completed ending with a WS row.
Patt note: The 3 smaller sizes have a panel of 4 ridges, whilst the 3 largest sizes have a panel of 5 ridges.
Working eyelet patt as set throughout, cont shaping sides as before on every foll 6th row to until to 57 (60: 63: 65: 68: 73) sts.
Work straight until front matches back to armhole shaping, ending with a WS row.

Shape armhole
Cast off 4 (4: 4: 5: 5: 5) sts at beg of next row. 53 (56: 59: 60: 63: 68) sts.
Work 1 row.
Dec 1 st at armhole edge on next 5 (7: 7: 7: 7: 11) rows, and 4 (3: 4: 4: 5: 4) foll alt rows ending with a **RS** row.
44 (46: 48: 49: 51: 53) sts.
Work 1 row.
Shape front neck
Next row (RS): Work until there are 30 (31: 32: 33: 35: 37) sts on right needle and turn, leaving rem 14 (15: 16: 16: 16: 16) sts on a holder.
Work each side of neck separately.
Dec 1 st at beg of next row.
29 (30: 31: 32: 34: 36) sts.
Next row (RS)(dec): Dec 1 st at each end of next row (this completes armhole shaping).
27 (28: 29: 30: 32: 34) sts.
Dec 1 st at neck edge on next 4 (4: 4: 4: 6: 6) rows, then on 3 (3: 3: 4: 3: 4) foll alt rows.
Work 3 rows.
Dec 1 st at neck edge on next row, then on foll 6th row, and then on foll 8th row.
17 (18: 19: 19: 20: 21) sts.
Work straight until front matches back to shoulder shaping, ending with a WS row.
Shape shoulder
Cast off 6 (6: 7: 7: 7: 7) sts at beg of next row and 6 (6: 6: 6: 7: 7) sts at beg of foll alt row.
Work 1 row. Cast off rem 5 (6: 6: 6: 6: 7) sts.
Mark the positions of 8 buttons (4 pairs); the first button to come on the second row of upper front, with the second one 8 rows above, the eighth will come 2 rows into neckband, with the seventh 8 rows below, the rem two pairs spaced evenly between, with each pair 8 rows apart.

CHART FOR BACK & FRONTS

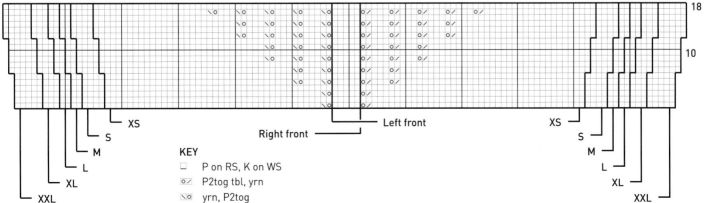

18
10

XS
S
M
L
XL
XXL

Right front
Left front

XS
S
M
L
XL
XXL

KEY
□ P on RS, K on WS
P2tog tbl, yrn
yrn, P2tog

RIGHT FRONT

Lower edging

Cast on 1 st using 3 ¼ mm (US 3) needles.

Shape front curve as folls:

Row 1 (RS): Inc in st. 2 sts.

Row 2: K1, inc in last st. 3 sts.

Row 3: Inc in first st, K2. 4 sts.

Row 4: K3, inc in last st. 5 sts.

Row 5: Inc in first st, K4. 6 sts.

Row 6: K5, inc in last st. 7 sts.

Row 7 (RS) (inc): Inc in first st, K1, yfwd, K2tog, K3. 8 sts.

Row 8 (inc): K5, inc in next st, K2. 9 sts.

Row 9 (inc): K2, inc in next st, K1, yfwd, K2tog, inc in each next 3 sts.

Row 10(inc): Cast off 3 sts, K until 5 sts on right needle, inc in next st, K4. 11 sts.

Row 11 (inc): K to last 7 sts, inc in next st, K1, yfwd, K2tog, K3. 12 sts.

Row 12: K until 5 sts on needle, yfwd, K2tog, K to end.

Now keeping the pattern correct and **at the same time** cont inc (as in row 11) on next row and every foll alt row to 19 (19: 19: 21: 21: 21) sts and then on every foll 4th row to 23 (23: 23: 25: 25: 25) sts.

Work straight in patt until right front edging matches left front edging to marker, ending with a WS row.

Shape side

Work as given for back from *** to ***.

Upper right front

With RS of lower edging facing and using 3 ¾ mm (US 5) needles, starting at **fasten off point**, pick up and knit 47 (50: 53: 55: 58: 63) sts across long straight edge, to cast off edge, turn and **knit** to end.

Cont in **rev st st**, setting stitch for front band and shaping sides as folls:

Next row (RS)(buttonhole row): K2, K2tog, yfwd, K2, P to end.

Next row: Knit.

Working 6 sts at centre front in garter st throughout, and working 6 more buttonholes as before, to correspond with markers on left front, cont as folls:

Work 0 (0: 2: 2: 2: 2) rows.

Next row (RS)(inc): K6, P to last 2 sts, M1p, P2. 48 (51: 54: 56: 59: 64) sts.

Work 5 rows.

Inc 1 st as before at beg of next row and foll 6th row. 50 (53: 56: 58: 61: 66) sts.

Work 5 rows, ending with a WS row.

Keeping buttonholes correct, cont from chart for right front, setting stitches for eyelet panel as folls:

Chart row 1 (RS)(inc): Work until there 11 sts on right needle, yrn, P2tog, P to last 2 sts, M1p, P2. 51 (54: 57: 59: 62: 67) sts.

Chart row 2: Knit.

Keeping side shaping correct cont until chart row 16 (16: 16: 18: 18: 18) has been completed ending with a WS row.

Complete as given for left front following chart for right front and working buttonholes as indicated.

SLEEVES (work both the same)

Cast on 95 (97: 99: 101: 103: 105) sts using 3 ¾ mm (US 5) needles and work beg with a **P** row cont in **rev st st** setting stitches for eyelet panel as folls:

Row 1 (RS): P39 (40: 41: 41: 42: 43), P2tog tbl, yrn, P2 (2: 2: 3: 3: 3), yrn, P2tog tbl, P5, yrn, P2tog, P2 (2: 2: 3: 3: 3), yrn, P2tog, P to end.

Row 2: Knit.

These 2 rows set the sts and form the eyelet patt and are rep throughout.

Work 4 rows.

Next row (RS)(dec): P2, P2tog, patt to last 4 sts, P2tog tbl, P2.

Work 5 rows.

Dec 1 st as before at each end of next row and 7 foll 6th rows, ending with a **RS** row. 77 (79: 81: 83: 85: 87) sts.

Work 11 rows.

Dec 1 st as before at each end of next row and foll 12th row.

73 (75: 77: 79: 81: 83) sts.

Work straight until sleeve measures 31 (32: 33: 34: 35: 36) cm, ending with a WS row.

Shape sleeve top

Cast off 4 (4: 4: 5: 5: 5) sts at beg of next 2 rows.

65 (67: 69: 69: 71: 73) sts.

Dec 1 st at each end of next 3 rows and foll alt row, and then on every foll 4th row to 47 (49: 51: 49: 49: 51) sts, end with a **RS** row.

Work 1 row.

Dec 1 st at each end of next row and 2 (4: 3: 2: 3: 4) foll alt rows, and then on every foll row to 31 (33: 33: 33: 35: 35) sts.

Cast off 3 sts at beg of next 2 rows.

Cast off rem 25 (27: 27: 27: 29: 29) sts.

Cuff

With RS of sleeve facing, cast off edge

uppermost and using 3mm (US 2/3) needles, pick up and knit 95 (97: 99: 101: 103: 105) sts across lower edge of sleeve.

Next row (WS): K1, (K2tog) to end.

48 (49: 50: 51: 52: 53) sts.

Knit 7 (7: 7: 9: 9: 9) rows, ending with a **RS** row.

Cast off knitwise (on WS).

MAKING UP

Join shoulder seams, using back stitch or mattress st if preferred.

Neck edging

With RS of right front facing and using 3 mm (US 2/3) needles, slip 14 (15: 16: 16: 16: 16) sts from holder onto right needle, rejoin yarn and pick up and knit 32 (34: 34: 36: 40: 40) sts up right front neck, 35 (37: 39: 41: 43: 45) sts across back and 32 (34: 34: 36: 40: 40) sts down left front neck, then K 14 (15: 16: 16: 16: 16) sts from holder.

127 (135: 139: 145: 155: 157) sts.

Next row (WS): Knit.

Next row (RS)(buttonhole): K2, K2tog, yfwd, K to end.

Knit 6 (6: 6: 8: 8: 8) rows.

Cast off knitwise (on WS).

Join side and sleeve seams.

Set sleeves into armholes.

Sew on buttons to correspond with buttonholes.

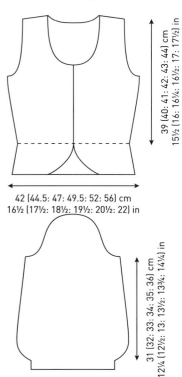

42 (44.5: 47: 49.5: 52: 56) cm
16½ (17½: 18½: 19½: 20½: 22) in

39 (40: 41: 42: 43: 44) cm
15½ (16: 16¼: 16½: 17: 17½) in

31 (32: 33: 34: 35: 36) cm
12¼ (12½: 13: 13½: 13¾: 14¼) in

HAVEN

A COSY SCARF WORKED IN PANELS OF LACE

Recommendation

Suitable for the knitter with a little experience.
Please see page 39 for photograph.

Size

One size

Rowan Cocoon

4 x 100gm

Needles

1 pair 8mm (no 0) (US 11) needles

Tension

14 sts and 17 rows to 10cm measured over
pattern using 8mm (no 0) (US 11) needles

Finished length

Approximately 28cm (11ins) wide and 202cm
(80ins) long

SCARF

Cast on 40 sts using 8mm (US 11) needles.
Next row (RS): Sl 1, K to end.
Rep this row 4 times more, ending with
a RS row.
Next row (WS): Sl 1, K2, P to last 3 sts, K3.
Cont in lace patt as folls:
Row 1 (RS): Sl 1, K2, K2tog, (K5, yfwd, K1,
yfwd, K2, sl 1, K2tog, psso) twice, K5, yfwd,
K1, yfwd, K2, sl 1, K1, psso, K3.
Row 2 & all WS rows: Sl 1, K2,
P to last 3 sts, K3.
Row 3: Sl 1, K2, K2tog, (K4, yfwd, K3, yfwd,
K1, sl 1, K2tog, psso) twice, K4, yfwd, K3,
yfwd, K1, sl 1, K1, psso, K3.
Row 5: Sl 1, K2, K2tog, (K3, yfwd, K5, yfwd,
sl 1, K2tog, psso) twice, K3, yfwd, K5, yfwd, sl
1, K1, psso, K3.
Row 7: Sl 1, K2, K2tog, (K2, yfwd, K1, yfwd,
K5, sl 1, K2tog, psso) twice, K2, yfwd, K1,
yfwd, K5, sl 1, K1, psso, K3.
Row 9: Sl 1, K2, K2tog, (K1, yfwd, K3, yfwd,
K4, sl 1, K2tog, psso) twice, K1, yfwd, K3,
yfwd, K4, sl 1, K1, psso, K3.
Row 11: Sl 1, K2, K2tog, (yfwd, K5, yfwd, K3,
sl 1, K2tog, psso) twice, yfwd, K5, yfwd, K3,
sl 1, K1, psso, K3.
Row 12 (WS): Sl 1, K2, P to last 3 sts, K3.
These 12 rows form the pattern and are
repeated throughout.
Work a further 27 patt reps, ending with
a WS row.
Next row (RS): Sl 1, K to end.
Rep this row 4 times more, ending with
a RS row.
Cast off knitwise (on WS).

Recommendation

Suitable for the more experienced knitter.
Please see page 43 for photograph.

	XS	S	M	L	XL	XXL	
To fit	81	86	91	97	102	109	cm
bust	32	34	36	38	40	43	in

Rowan Kid Classic

| | 4 | 5 | 5 | 6 | 6 | 7 | x 50gm |

Needles

1 pair 4mm (no 8) (US 6) needles
1 pair 4 ½ mm (no 7) (US 7) needles

Tension

21 sts and 27 rows to 10cm measured over
reversed stocking stitch using 4 ½ mm (US 7)
needles

NIGHTSHADE
ASYMETRIC PONCHO WITH A SLOUCHY NECKLINE & CORSAGE

BACK (Worked from neck downwards)
Using 4 ½ mm (US 7) needles cast on as folls:
Cast-on 1 st onto left needle, *insert right
needle into loop, wrap yarn around needle
and bring loop through as if knitting a stitch
but leave the stitch on left needle, (wrap the
yarn around the right needle and bring loop
through) 4 times making a short chain,
place this last loop on the left needle; rep
from * until 53 (57: 57: 57: 61: 63) sts on
left needle.
Beg with a **P** row, cont in rev st st.
Work 24 (26: 26: 26: 28: 28) rows, ending
with a RS row.

Shape shoulders and side seam
Cast on 5 (5: 6: 7: 7: 8) sts at beg of next
2 rows and 3 (3: 3: 3: 4: 5) sts at beg of foll
2 rows. 69 (73: 75: 77: 83: 89) sts.
Inc 1 st at each end of next and every foll row to
81 (85: 91: 97: 107: 113) sts, end with a WS row.
Inc 1 st at each end of next row and every foll
alt row to 109 (111: 113: 117: 121: 127) sts,
ending with a **RS** row.
Work 3 rows.
Inc 1 st at each end of next row, then on
3 (4: 3: 3: 4: 4) foll 4th rows and then on
0 (0: 2: 2: 2: 2) foll 6th rows.
117 (121: 125: 129: 135: 141) sts.
Cont until work measures 30 (32: 33: 34:
36: 38)cm from cast on edge, ending with
a **RS** row. **
Next row (WS)(inc): Knit to end, turn and cast
on 7 sts. 124 (128: 132: 136: 142: 148) sts.
Work frill edge and shape lower edge
*** Row 1 (RS)(dec): K1, (take yarn around
needle and draw yarn through loop on right
needle) 4 times (to create a short chain),
K6, P3tog, P to end.
122 (126: 130: 134: 140: 146) sts.
Row 2: Knit to last 9 sts, K2tog, K7.
121 (125: 129: 133: 139: 145) sts.
Row 3: Work as row 1.
Row 4: Work as row 2.
118 (122: 126: 130: 136: 142) sts.
Rep from *** twice more.
106 (110: 114: 118: 124: 130) sts.

Next row (RS): Work 7 sts, P3tog, P to end,
turn and cast on 7 sts.
111 (115: 119: 123: 129: 135) sts.
Next row (WS): Work 7 sts as row 1, K2tog
tbl, K to last 9 sts, K2tog, K7.
109 (113: 117: 121: 127: 133) sts.
Keeping the loop edging correct on both
edges cont as folls:
****Short row shaping rows: Work 6 sts,
wrap next st (by slipping next st to right
needle, taking yarn to opposite side of work
between needles and then slipping same st
back onto left needle – when working back
across sts work the loop tog with the wrapped
st), turn and K to end.
Row 1 (RS): Work 7 sts, P3tog, P to last 9 sts,
P2tog tbl, K7.
Short row shaping rows: Work 6 sts, wrap
next st, turn and K to end.
Row 2: Work 7 sts, K2tog tbl, K to last 9 sts,
K2tog, K7.
Row 3: Work as row 1.
Row 4: Work as row 2.
Rep from **** until 19 (18: 17: 16: 17: 18)
sts rem, ending with row 4 (2: 4: 2: 4: 2) and
a WS row.
***** Next row (RS): Work 7 sts, with yarn at
front, **for XS only,** sl 1, P4tog, psso, **for S and
XXL sizes only,** sl 1, P3tog, psso, **for M and
XL sizes only,** sl 1, P2tog, psso, **for L size
only,** P2tog, **all sizes** K7.
15 sts.
Next row (WS): Work 6 sts, wrap next st,
turn and K to end.
Rep the last row 3 times more.
Next row (WS): Work 7 sts, K to end.
Next row (RS): Work 6 sts, wrap next st,
turn and K to end.
Rep the last row 3 times more.
Next row: K6, P3tog, K6.
Cast off rem 13 sts.

FRONT
Work as for back to **.
Next row (WS)(inc): Cast on 7 sts, K to end.
124 (128: 132: 136: 142: 148) sts.

Work frill edge and shape lower edge

*** Row 1(RS)(dec): P to last 10 sts, P3tog tbl, K7.

122 (126: 130: 134: 140: 146) sts.

Row 2: K1, (take yarn around needle and draw yarn through loop on right needle) 4 times, K6 (7 sts on needle), K2tog tbl, K to end.

121 (125: 129: 133: 139: 145) sts.

Row 3: Work as row 1.

Short row shaping rows: Work 6 sts, wrap next st, turn and K to end.

Row 4: Work as row 2.

118 (122: 126: 130: 136: 142) sts.

Rep from *** twice more.

106 (110: 114: 118: 124: 130) sts.

Next row (RS): Cast on and knit 7 sts, P to last 10 sts, P3tog tbl, K7.

111 (115: 119: 123: 129: 135) sts.

Next row (WS): Work 7 sts, K2tog tbl, K to last 9 sts, K2tog, K7.

109 (113: 117: 121: 127: 133) sts.

Keeping the loop edging correct on both edges cont as folls:

**** Short row shaping rows: Work 6 sts, wrap next st, turn and K to end.

Row 1 (RS): Work 7 sts, P2tog, P to last 10 sts, P3tog tbl, K7.

Short row shaping rows: Work 6 sts, wrap next st, turn and K to end.

Row 2: Work 7 sts, K2tog tbl, K to last 9 sts, K2tog, K7.

Row 3: Work as row 1.

Row 4: Work as row 2.

Rep from **** until 19 (18: 17: 16: 17: 18) sts rem, ending with row 4 (2: 4: 2: 4: 2) and a WS row.

Complete as given for back, from *****.

MAKING UP

Press both pieces as described on the information page.

Join shoulder and side seams using back stitch, or mattress st if preferred.

Corsage

Inner circle

Cast on 6 sts using 4mm (US 6) needles.

**Row 1 (RS): K1, (take yarn around needle and draw yarn through loop on right needle) 4 times, K to end.

Row 2: Knit.

Working the loop edging on all RS rows, cont as folls:

Rows 3 & 4 (short row shaping rows): Work 4 sts, wrap next st, turn and K to end.

Rows 5 & 6 (short row shaping rows): Work as rows 3 & 4.

Rep from ** 9 times more.

Cast off.

Sew the cast-on and cast-off edges together to form a circle.

Work a running stitch around the inside edge, draw up tightly and fasten off.

Rejoin yarn and work a second row of running stitches approx 1cm up from centre.

Draw up and fasten off.

Outer circle

Cast on 8 sts using 4mm (US 6) needles.

**Row 1 (RS): K1, (take yarn around needle and draw yarn through loop on right needle) 4 times, K to end.

Row 2: Knit.

Working the loop edging on all RS rows cont as folls:

Rows 3 & 4 (short row shaping rows): Work 4 sts, wrap next st, turn and K to end.

Rows 5 & 6 (short row shaping rows): Work 6 sts, wrap next st, turn and K to end.

Rep from ** 19 times more.

Cast off.

Sew the cast-on and cast-off edges together to form a circle.

Work a running stitch around the inside edge, draw up tightly and fasten off.

Rejoin yarn and work a second row of running stitches approx 1cm up from centre.

Place the inner circle on top of the outer circle.

Draw up second row of running stitches on the outer circle around the base of the inner circle and fasten off, then using the same yarn slip stitch the two circles together.

Sew securely in place as in photograph.

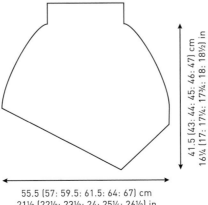

41.5 (43: 44: 45: 46: 47) cm
16¼ (17: 17¼: 17¾: 18: 18½) in

55.5 (57: 59.5: 61.5: 64: 67) cm
21½ (22½: 23½: 24: 25¼: 26½) in

ERIN

CABLE CARDIGAN WITH CONTRASTING BUTTON DETAIL

Recommendation

Suitable for the knitter with a little experience.
Please see pages 44 & 45 for photographs.

	XS	S	M	L	XL	XXL	
To fit	**81**	**86**	**91**	**97**	**102**	**109**	**cm**
bust	32	34	36	38	40	43	in

Rowan Calmer

	8	9	9	9	10	11	x 50gm

Buttons 7

Needles

1 pair 4mm (no 8) (US 6) needles
1 pair 4 ½ mm (no 7) (US 7) needles
1 pair 5mm (no 6) (US 8) needles
Cable needle

Tension

21 sts and 30 rows to 10cm over reversed
stocking stitch using 5 mm (US 8) needles

Special abbreviations

C6B = slip next 3 sts onto cable needle and
leave at back of work, K3, then K3 from cable
needle.
C6F = slip next 3 sts onto cable needle and
leave at front of work, K3, then K3 from cable
needle.

BACK

Cast on 159 (177: 183: 189: 207: 215) sts
using 5mm (US 8) needles and work lower
edging in moss st as folls:
Row 1 (RS): (K1, P1) to last st, K1.
Row 2: Work as row 1.
These 2 rows form moss st.
Rep the last 2 rows once more.
Next row (RS): Moss st 8 (2: 5: 8: 2: 6), (K8,
moss st 7) to last 16 (10: 13: 16: 10: 14) sts,
K8, moss st 8 (2: 5: 8: 2: 6).
Next row: Moss st 8 (2: 5: 8: 2: 6), (P8, moss
st 7) to last 16 (10: 13: 16: 10: 14) sts, P8,
moss st 8 (2: 5: 8: 2: 6).
Rep the last 2 rows once more.
Next row (RS): P8 (2: 5: 8: 2: 6), (K8, P7) to
last 16 (10: 13: 16: 10: 14) sts, K8, P to end.
Next row: K8 (2: 5: 8: 2: 6), (P8, K7) to last
16 (10: 13: 16: 10: 14) sts, P8, K to end.
Rep these last 2 rows until back measures
14cm, ending with a **RS** row. ***
Next row (WS)(dec): K8 (2: 5: 8: 2: 6), (P2tog
tbl, P4, P2tog, K2tog, K3, K2tog tbl) to last
16 (10: 13: 16: 10: 14) sts, P2tog tbl, P4,
P2tog, K to end.
121 (131: 137: 143: 153: 161) sts.
Next row (RS)(cable row): P8 (2: 5: 8: 2: 6),
(C6B, P5) 5 (6: 6: 6: 7: 7) times, (C6F, P5)
4 (5: 5: 5: 6: 6) times, C6F, P to end.
Work 11 rows in rib.
The last 12 rows form the cable rib patt
and are rep throughout.
Keeping cable patt correct throughout
cont until back measures 31 (31: 32:
32: 33: 33)cm, ending with a WS row.
Shape armholes
Cast off 6 sts at beg of next 2 rows.
109 (119: 125: 131: 141: 149) sts.
Dec 1 st at each end of next 5 (9: 11: 7:
11: 13) rows and then every foll alt row to
93 (97: 99: 113: 115: 117) sts, ending with
a RS row.
Work 3 rows.
Dec 1 st at each end of next row and foll
4th row.
89 (93: 95: 109: 111: 113) sts.

Work straight until armhole measures
18 (19: 19: 20: 21: 22)cm, ending with
a WS row.
Shape shoulders and back neck
Cast off 8 (8: 8: 10: 10: 10) sts at beg of
next 2 rows. 73 (77: 79: 89: 91: 93) sts.
Cast off 7 (8: 8: 10: 10: 10), patt until there
are 11 (11: 11: 13: 13: 13) sts on right needle
and turn, leaving rem sts on a holder.
Work each side of neck separately.
Cast off 4 sts at beg of next row.
Cast off rem 7 (7: 7: 9: 9: 9) sts.
With RS facing rejoin yarn to rem sts, cast off
centre 37 (39: 41: 43: 45: 47) sts, work
to end.
Complete to match first side, reversing
shaping.

LEFT FRONT

Cast on 86 (95: 98: 101: 110: 114) sts using
using 5mm (US 8) needles and work lower
edging in moss st as folls:
Row 1 (RS): K0 (1: 0: 1: 0: 0), (P1, K1)
to end.
Row 2: (K1, P1) 4 times, K3, (P1, K1) to
last 1 (0: 1: 0: 1: 1) st, P1 (0: 1: 0: 1: 1).
Rep the last 2 rows once more.
Next row (RS): Moss st 8 (2: 5: 8: 2: 6), (K8,
moss st 7) to last 18 sts, K8, P1, moss st 9.
Next row: Moss st 9, K1, (P8, moss st 7) to
last 16 (10: 13: 16: 10: 14) sts, P8, moss st
8 (2: 5: 8: 2: 6).
Rep the last 2 rows once more.
Next row (RS): P8 (2: 5: 8: 2: 6), (K8, P7)
to last 18 sts, K8, P1, moss st 9.
Next row: Moss st 9, K1, (P8, K7) to last
16 (10: 13: 16: 10: 14) sts, P8, K to end.
Rep these last 2 rows until left front matches
back to ***.
Next row (WS)(dec): Patt 10, (P2tog tbl, P4,
P2tog, K2tog, K3, K2tog tbl) to last 16 (10:
13: 16: 10: 14) sts, P2tog tbl, P4, P2tog, K
to end. 68 (73: 76: 79: 84: 88) sts.
Next row (RS)(cable row): P8 (2: 5: 8: 2: 6),
(C6B, P5) to last 16 sts, C6B, patt 10.
Work 11 rows on sts as set.

The last 12 rows form the cable rib patt and are rep throughout. Keeping cable patt and front edge stitches correct throughout cont until left front matches back to armhole shaping, ending with a WS row.

Shape armhole
Cast off 6 sts at beg of next row.
62 (67: 70: 73: 78: 82) sts.
Work 1 row.
Dec 1 st at armhole edge on next 5 (9: 11: 7: 11: 13) rows and then every foll alt row to 54 (56: 57: 64: 65: 66) sts, end with a RS row.
Work 3 rows.
Dec 1 st at armhole edge on next row and foll 4th row. 52 (54: 55: 62: 63: 64) sts.
Work straight until front is 20 (20: 22: 24: 26: 26) rows shorter than back to beg of shoulder shaping, ending with a WS row.

Shape front neck
Next row (RS): Patt 32 (33: 33: 40: 42: 42) sts and turn, leaving rem 20 (21: 22: 22: 21: 22) sts on a holder for neck edging.
Dec 1 st at neck edge on next 6 (6: 6: 6: 8: 8) rows, then on 2 (2: 2: 3: 3: 3) foll alt rows, and then on 2 foll 4th rows.
22 (23: 23: 29: 29: 29) sts.
Work 1 (1: 3: 3: 3: 3) rows, end with a WS row.

Shape shoulder
Cast off 8 (8: 8: 10: 10: 10) sts at beg of next row and 7 (8: 8: 10: 10: 10) sts at beg of foll alt row.
Work 1 row.
Cast off rem 7 (7: 7: 9: 9: 9) sts.
Mark position of 7 buttonholes, first to come opposite first cable, the seventh will come 2 rows into neck edging and rem 5 spaced evenly between.

RIGHT FRONT
Cast on 86 (95: 98: 101: 110: 114) sts using using 5mm (US 8) needles and work lower edging in moss st as folls:
Row 1 (RS): (K1, P1) to last 0 (1: 0: 1: 0: 0) st, K0 (1: 0: 1: 0: 0).
Row 2: P1 (0: 1: 0: 1: 1), (K1, P1) to last 11 sts, K3, (P1, K1) to end.
Rep the last 2 rows once more.
Next row (RS): Patt 10, (K8, moss st 7) to last 16 (10: 13: 16: 10: 14) sts, K8, moss st 8 (2: 5: 8: 2: 6).
Next row: Moss st 8 (2: 5: 8: 2: 6), (P8, moss st 7) to last 18 sts, P8, K1, moss st 9.
Rep the last 2 rows once more.

Next row (RS): Moss st 10, (K8, P7) to last 16 (10: 13: 16: 10: 14) sts, K8, P8 (2: 5: 8: 2: 8).
Next row: K8 (2: 5: 8: 2: 6), (P8, K7) to last 18 sts, P8, K1, moss st 9.
Rep these last 2 rows until right front matches back to ***.
Next row (WS)(dec): K8 (2: 5: 8: 2: 6), (P2tog tbl, P4, P2tog, K2tog, K3, K2tog tbl) to last 18 sts, P2tog tbl, P4, P2tog, patt 10.
68 (73: 76: 79: 84: 88) sts.
Next row (RS)(cable)(buttonhole): Patt 4, patt 2 tog, yon, patt 3, P1, (C6F, P5) to last 14 (8: 11: 14: 8: 12) sts, C6F, P8 (2: 5: 8: 2: 6).
Work 11 rows on sts as set.
The last 12 rows form the cable rib patt and are rep throughout.
Complete to match left front, rev shapings and working buttonholes as before to correspond with positions marked for buttons.

SLEEVES (work both the same)
Cast on 47 (49: 51: 53: 55: 57) sts using 4 ½ mm (US 7) needles and work in moss st as folls:
Row 1 (RS): K1, (P1, K1) to end.
Row 2: Work as row 1.
These 2 rows form moss st.
Work 12 more rows.
Change to 5mm (US 8) needles and cont in rev st st, shaping sides as folls:
Beg with a P row, work 2 rows in rev st st.
Next row (RS)(inc): P2, M1p, P to last 2 sts, M1p, P2. 49 (51: 53: 55: 57: 59) sts.
Work 15 rows.
Inc 1 st as before at each end of next row and 2 (2: 2: 4: 4: 4) foll 16th rows, and then every foll 14th row to 63 (65: 67: 69: 71: 73) sts.
Work straight until sleeve measures 43 (44: 45: 46: 47: 48)cm, ending with a WS row.

Shape top
Please note: To compensate for the cables worked on the body, less sts are cast off at this point than on the back and fronts.
Cast off 4 sts at beg of next 2 rows.
55 (57: 59: 61: 63: 65) sts.
Dec 1 st at each end of next 3 rows and foll alt row, and then on every foll 4th row to 39 (39: 41: 41: 43: 45) sts, ending with a RS row.
Work 1 row.
Dec 1 st at each end of next row and 2 (4: 4: 3: 4: 5) foll alt rows and then every foll row to 23 (23: 25: 27: 27: 27) sts, ending with a WS row.
Cast off 3 sts at beg of next 2 rows.
Cast off rem 17 (17: 19: 21: 21: 21) sts.

MAKING UP
Pin the pieces out and steam.
Join shoulder seams, using back stitch or mattress st if preferred.

Neck edging
With RS of right front facing and using 4mm (US 6) needles, slip 20 (21: 22: 22: 21: 22) sts from holder onto **left** needle, slip first 10 of these stitches onto right needle, rejoin yarn and (K2tog) 3 times, P4 (5: 6: 6: 5: 6), pick up and knit 20 (20: 22: 24: 26: 26) sts up right front neck, 33 (35: 37: 39: 41: 43) sts across back and 20 (20: 22: 24: 26: 26) sts down left front, work across 20 (21: 22: 22: 21: 22) sts on holder as folls: P4 (5: 6: 6: 5: 6), (K2tog) 3 times, patt to end. 107 (111: 119: 125: 129: 133) sts.
Next row (WS): Patt 10, moss st to last 10 sts, patt to end.
Rep this row twice more.
Next row (RS)(buttonhole): Patt 4, patt 2 tog, yon, patt 3, P1, patt to end.
Work 4 more rows.
Cast off in patt.
Join side and sleeve seams.
Set sleeves into armholes.
Sew on buttons to correspond with buttonholes.

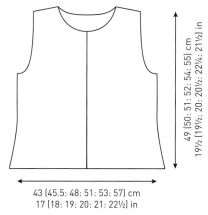

49 (50: 51: 52: 54: 55] cm
19½ (19½: 20: 20½: 22¼: 21½] in

43 (45.5: 48: 51: 53: 57] cm
17 (18: 19: 20: 21: 22½] in

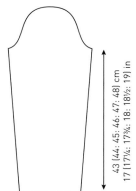

43 (44: 45: 46: 47: 48] cm
17 (17¼: 17¾: 18: 18½: 19] in

Recommendation

Suitable for the knitter with a little experience.
Please see page 46 – 48 for photographs.

	XS	S	M	L	XL	XXL	
To fit	**81**	**86**	**91**	**97**	**102**	**109**	**cm**
bust	32	34	36	38	40	43	in

Rowan Big Wool

| | 4 | 4 | 5 | 5 | 5 | 6 | x100gm |

Needles

1 pair 12mm (US 17) needles

Button 1

Tension

8 sts and 12 rows to 10cm measured over
stocking stitch using 12mm (US 17) needles.

Special abbreviation

MP = Make picot: cast on 1 st, cast off 1 st.

CHERISH

FITTED SHRUG WITH SINGLE BUTTON FASTENING

BACK

Lower edging (knitted from side to side)
Cast on 7 (8: 8: 8: 9: 9) sts using 12mm
(US 17) needles.
Row 1 (RS): MP, K to end
Row 2: Knit.
Rep these 2 rows until 40 (44: 46: 50: 52: 56)
rows have been completed, ending with
a WS row.
Cast off, but do not break the yarn.

Upper back

With RS of lower eding facing and using
12mm (US 17) needles, pick up and knit
29 (31: 33: 35: 37: 41) sts evenly along the
top (straight) edge of edging and purl 1 row,
ending with a WS row.
Beg with a K row, cont in st st as folls:
Work 4 rows.
Next row (RS) (inc): K2, M1, K to last 2 sts,
M1, K2.
31 (33: 35: 37: 39: 43) sts.
Work 3 (3: 5: 5: 5: 5) rows, ending with
a WS row.

Shape armholes

Cast off 2 sts at beg of next 2 rows.
27 (29: 31: 33: 35: 39) sts.
Dec 1 st at each end of next 2 (2: 2: 2: 3: 3)
rows and 0 (0: 0: 1: 0: 2) foll alt rows.
23 (25: 27: 27: 29: 29) sts.
Work 14 (16: 16: 17: 15) rows, ending with
a WS row.

Shape back neck and shoulders

Knit 7 (7: 8: 8: 8: 8) sts and turn, leaving rem
sts on a holder.
Work each side of neck separately.
Next row (WS): Dec 1 st at neck edge on
next row.
6 (6: 7: 7: 7: 7) sts.
Next row: Cast off 3 sts at beg and dec 1 st
at end of row. 2 (2: 3: 3: 3: 3) sts.
Work 1 row.
Cast off.
With RS facing rejoin yarn to rem sts, cast off
centre 9 (11: 11: 11: 13: 13) sts, K to end.
Complete to match first side reversing
shaping.

LEFT FRONT

**Lower edging (knitted from side seam to
centre front)**
Cast on 7 (8: 8: 8: 9: 9) sts using 12mm
(US 17) needles.
Row 1 (RS): Knit.
Row 2: MP, K to end.
Rep these 2 rows until 22 (24: 26: 28: 30: 32)
rows have been completed, ending with
a WS row.
Break yarn, leaving sts on needle.

Upper left front

With RS of lower edging facing, pick up and
knit 14 (15: 16: 17: 18: 20) sts evenly along
the top (straight) edge of the lower edging,
then K across 7 (8: 8: 8: 9: 9) sts of
lower edging. 21 (23: 24: 25: 27: 29) sts.
Next row (WS): MP, K until 7 (8: 8: 8: 9: 9) sts
on right needle, P to end.

Shape lower edge

Short row shaping (RS): K10 (11: 12: 13: 14:
16) sts, wrap next stitch (by slipping next st
to right needle, taking yarn to opposite side
of work between needles and then slipping
same st back onto left needle – when working
back across sts work the wrapped loop tog
with the wrapped st), turn and Purl to end.
Short row shaping (RS): K12 (13: 14: 15: 16:
18) sts, wrap next stitch, turn and purl to end.
Next row (RS)(inc): K2, M1, K to end.
22 (24: 25: 26: 28: 30) sts.
Next row: MP, K until 7 (8: 8: 8: 9: 9) sts on
right needle, P to end.
These 2 rows set the stitches.
Work 2 rows.

Shape armhole and front neck

Next row (RS)(dec): Cast off 2 sts, K until
9 (10: 10: 10: 11: 11) sts rem on **left** needle,
K2tog tbl, K to end. 19 (21: 22: 23: 25: 27) sts.
Work 1 row.
Dec 1 st at armhole edge on next 2 (2: 2: 2: 3:
3) rows and 0 (0: 0: 1: 0: 2) foll alt rows, **and
at the same time** dec 1 st as before on front
front edge on next row and 2 (2: 2: 2: 3: 3) foll
alt rows. 14 (16: 17: 17: 18: 18) sts.
Work 3 rows.

Dec 1 st as before at front edge, on next row and every foll 4th row until 12 (13: 14: 14: 15: 15) sts rem, ending with a RS row.
Work 5 (3: 3: 5: 3: 5) rows, ending with a WS row.

Shape shoulder

Cast off 3 sts at beg of next row.
Work 1 row.
Cast off 2 (2: 3: 3: 3: 3) inc in next st, K to end. 8 (9: 9: 9: 10: 10) sts.
Cont on these sts for a further 8 (10: 10: 10: 12: 12) rows.
Cast off.

RIGHT FRONT

Lower edging (knitted from side seam to centre)

Cast on 7 (8: 8: 8: 9: 9) sts using 12mm (US 17) needles.
Row 1 (RS): MP, K to end.
Row 2: Knit.
Rep these 2 rows until 23 (25: 27: 29: 31: 33) rows have been completed, end with a **RS** row.
Do not cast off or break yarn.

Upper right front

With RS facing pick up and knit 14 (15: 16: 17: 18: 20) sts evenly along the top (straight) edge of lower edging.
21 (23: 24: 25: 27: 29) sts.

Shape lower edge

Short row shaping (WS): P10 (11: 12: 13: 14: 16) sts, wrap next stitch, turn and knit to end.
Short row shaping (WS): P12 (13: 14: 15: 16: 18) sts, wrap next stitch, turn and knit to end.
Next row (WS): P to last 7 (8: 8: 8: 9: 9) sts, K to end.
Next row (RS): MP, K to last 2 sts, M1, K2. 22 (24: 25: 26: 28: 30) sts.
Next row: P to last 7 (8: 8: 8: 9: 9) sts, K to end.
Next row (RS)(buttonhole): MP, K until 2 sts on right needle, K2tog tbl, (yon) twice, K2tog, K to end.
Next row: P to last 7 (8: 8: 8: 9: 9) sts, K to end, knitting back of loops made on previous row.
These last 2 rows set the stitches.
Omitting buttonhole, rep the last 2 rows 0 (0: 1: 1: 1: 1) times more, ending with a WS row.

Shape front neck and armhole

Next row (RS): MP, K until 7 (8: 8: 8: 9: 9) sts on right needle, K2tog, K to end. 21 (23: 24: 25: 27: 29) sts.

Cast off 2 sts at beg of next row, work to end. 19 (21: 22: 23: 25: 27) sts.
Dec 1 st at armhole edge on next 2 (2: 2: 2: 3: 3) rows and 0 (0: 0: 1: 0: 2) foll alt rows **and at the same time** dec 1 st at front edge on next row and 2 (2: 2: 2: 3: 3) foll alt rows. 14 (16: 17: 17: 18: 18) sts.
Complete to match left front, reversing shaping.

SLEEVES (both alike)

*Lower edging (knitted from side to side)

Cast on 7 (8: 8: 8: 9: 9) sts using 12mm (US 17) needles.

Shape side edge

Next row (RS): MP, K until 2 (3: 3: 3: 4: 4) sts on right needle, wrap next stitch, turn and K to end.
Next row: MP, K until 5 (6: 6: 6: 7: 7) sts on right needle, wrap next stitch, turn and K to end.
Working a picot at beg of every RS row, cont in garter st for a further 34 (36: 38: 38: 40: 42) rows, ending with a WS row.

Shape side edge

Next row: MP, K until 5 (6: 6: 6: 7: 7) sts on right needle, wrap next stitch, turn and K to end.
Next row: MP K until 2 (3: 3: 3: 4: 4) sts on right needle, wrap next stitch, turn and K to end.
Cast off, but do not break yarn.

Upper sleeve

With RS of lower edging facing and using 12mm (US 17) needles, pick up and knit 20 (21: 22: 23: 24: 25) sts evenly along the top (straight) edge of edging and purl 1 row, ending with a WS row.
Beg with a K row, cont in st st as folls:
Work 2 rows.
Next row (RS)(dec): K2, K2tog, K to last 4 sts, K2tog tbl, K2. 18 (19: 20: 21: 22: 23) sts.
Work 9 (9: 9: 9: 11: 11) rows, ending with a WS row.
Next row (RS)(inc): K2, M1, K to last 2 sts, M1, K2.
20 (21: 22: 23: 24: 25) sts.
Work 9 rows, ending with a WS row.
Inc as before at each end of next row and foll 10th row.
24 (25: 26: 27: 28: 29) sts.
Cont straight until sleeve measures 44 (45: 46: 47: 48: 49) cm, ending with a WS row.

Shape sleeve top

Cast off 2 sts at beg of next 2 rows. 20 (21: 22: 23: 24: 25) sts.
Work 0 (0: 0: 0: 0: 2) rows.
Dec 1 st at each end of next row.
18 (19: 20: 21: 22: 23) sts.
Work 3 rows.
Dec 1 st at each end of next row, then on 1 (1: 1: 2: 2: 2) foll 4th rows.
14 (15: 16: 15: 16: 17) sts.
Work 1 row.
Dec 1 st at each end of next row, then on 1 (1: 1: 0: 0: 0) foll alt row, then on every foll row until 8 (9: 10: 11: 12: 13) sts rem.
Cast off.

MAKING UP

Press all pieces as described on the information page.
Join both shoulder seams using back stitch or mattress stitch if preferred.
Join side and sleeve seams.
Set sleeve into armhole.
Join cast-off edge of the extended front band neatly together and sew into place around back neck.
Sew on button.

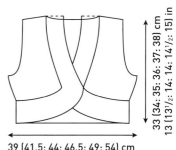

39 (41.5: 44: 46.5: 49: 54) cm
15¹/₂ (16¹/₂: 17¹/₂: 18¹/₂: 19¹/₂: 21¹/₂) in

33 [34: 35: 36: 37: 38] cm
13 (13¹/₂: 14: 14: 14¹/₂: 15] in

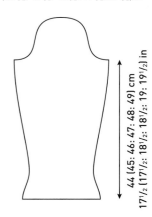

44 (45: 46: 47: 48: 49) cm
17¹/₂ (17¹/₂: 18¹/₂: 18¹/₂: 19: 19¹/₂) in

INFORMATION
A GUIDE TO ASSIST WITH TECHNIQUES & FINISHING TOUCHES

TENSION

Achieving the correct tension has to be one of the most important elements in producing a beautiful, well fitting knitted garment. The tension controls the size and shape of your finished piece and any variation to either stitches or rows, however slight, will affect your work and change the fit completely.

To avoid any disappointment, we would always recommend that you knit a tension square in the yarn and stitch given in the pattern, working perhaps four or five more stitches and rows than those given in the tension note.

When counting the tension, place your knitting on a flat surface and mark out a 10cm square with pins. Count the stitches between the pins. If you have too many stitches to 10cm your knitting it too tight, try again using thicker needles, if you have too few stitches to 10cm your knitting is too loose, so try again using finer needles. Please note, if you are unable to achieve the correct stitches and rows required, the stitches are more crucial as many patterns are knitted to length.
Keep an eye on your tension during knitting, especially if you're going back to work which has been put to one side for any length of time.

SIZING

The instructions are given for the smallest size. Where they vary, work the figures in brackets for the larger sizes. One set of figures refers to all sizes. The size diagram with each pattern will help you decide which size to knit. The measurements given on the size diagram are the actual size your garment should be when completed. Measurements will vary from design to design because the necessary ease allowances have been made in each pattern to give your garment the correct fit, i.e. a loose fitting garment will be several cm wider than a neat fitted one, a snug fitting garment may have no ease at all.

ABBREVIATIONS

K	knit
P	purl
st(s)	stitch(es)
inc	increas(e)(ing)
dec	decreas(e)(ing)
st st	stocking stitch (1 row K, 1 row P)
garter st	garter stitch (K every row)
beg	begin(ning)
foll	following
rem	remain(ing)
rev st st	reverse stocking stitch (1 row P, 1 row K)
rep	repeat
alt	alternate
cont	continue
patt	pattern
tog	together
mm	millimetres
cm	centimetres
in(s)	inch(es)
RS	right side
WS	wrong side
sl 1	slip one stitch
psso	pass slipped stitch over
tbl	through back of loop
M1	make one stitch by picking up horizontal loop before next stitch and knitting into back of it
M1p	make one stitch by picking up horizontal loop before next stitch and purling into back of it
yfwd	yarn forward
yon	yarn over needle
yrn	yarn round needle
Mp	Make picot: Cast on 1 st, by inserting the right needle between the first and second stitch on left needle, take yarn round needle, bring loop through and place on left (one stitch cast on), cast off 1 st, by knitting first the loop and then the next stitch, pass the first stitch over the second (one stitch cast off).

CROCHET

We are aware that crochet terminology varies from country to country. Please note we have used the English style in this publication.

Crochet abbreviations

ch	chain
ss	slip stitch
dc	double crochet
htr	half treble
tr	treble
dtr	double treble
htr2tog	half treble 2tog
tr2tog	treble 2tog
yoh	yarn over hook
sp(s)	space(s)

Double crochet

1 Insert the hook into the work (as indicated in the pattern), wrap the yarn over the hook and draw the yarn through the work only.
2 Wrap the yarn again and draw the yarn through both loops on the hook.
3 1 dc made

Half treble

1 Wrap the yarn over the hook and insert the hook into the work (as indicated in the pattern).
2 Wrap the yarn over the hook draw through the work only and wrap the yarn again.
3 Draw through all 3 loops on the hook.
4 1 half treble made.

Treble

1 Wrap the yarn over the hook and insert the hook into the work (as indicated on the pattern).
2 Wrap the yarn over the hook draw through the work only and wrap the yarn again.
3 Draw through the first 2 loops only and wrap the yarn again.
4 Draw through the last 2 loops on the hook.
5 1 treble made.

Double treble

1 Wrap the yarn over the hook twice and insert the hook into the work (as indicated in the pattern).
2 Wrap the yarn over the hook, draw through the work only and wrap the yarn again.
3 Draw through first 2 loops only and wrap the yarn again.
4 Draw through the next 2 loops only and wrap the yarn again.
5 Draw through the last 2 loops on the hook.
6 1 double treble made.

WRAP STITCH

A wrap stitch is used to eliminate the hole created when using the short row shaping method.
Work to the position on the row indicated in the pattern, wrap the next st (by slipping next st onto right needle, taking yarn to opposite side of work between needles and then slipping same st back onto left needle – on foll rows, K tog the loop and the wrapped st) and turn, cont from pattern.

BEADING

Bead 1 (RS rows) – place a bead by bringing yarn to front (RS) of work and slipping bead up next to st just worked, slip next st purlwise from left needle to right needle and return yarn to back (WS) of work, leaving bead sitting in front of slipped st on RS. Do not place beads on edge sts of rows as this will interfere with seaming and picking up sts.

Beading note

Before starting to knit, thread beads onto yarn. To do this, thread a fine sewing needle (one which will easily pass through the beads) with sewing thread. Knot ends of thread and then pass end of yarn through this loop. Thread a bead onto sewing thread and then gently slide it along and onto knitting yarn. Continue in this way until required numbers of beads are on yarn.

CHART NOTE

Some of our patterns include a chart. Each square on a chart represent a stitch and each line of squares a row of knitting.

When working from a chart, unless otherwise stated, read odd rows (RS) from right to left and even rows (WS) from left to right. The key alongside each chart indicates how each stitch is worked.

WORKING A LACE PATTERN

When working a lace pattern it is important to remember that if you are unable to work a full repeat i.e. both the increase and corresponding decrease and vice versa, the stitches should be worked in stocking stitch or an alternative stitch suggested in the pattern.

FINISHING INSTRUCTIONS

It is the pressing and finishing which will transform your knitted pieces into a garment to be proud of.

Pressing

Darn in ends neatly along the selvage edge. Follow closely any special instructions given on the pattern or ball band and always take great care not to over press your work.

Block out your knitting on a pressing or ironing board, easing into shape, and unless otherwise states, press each piece using a warm iron over a damp cloth.

Tip: Attention should be given to ribs/ edgings; if the garment is close fitting – steam the ribs gently so that the stitches fill out but stay elastic. Alternatively if the garment is to hang straight then steam out to the correct shape.

Tip: Take special care to press the selvages, as this will make sewing up both easier and neater.

CONSTRUCTION
Stitching together

When stitching the pieces together, remember to match areas of pattern very carefully where they meet. Use a stitch such as back stitch or mattress stitch for all main knitting seams and join all ribs and neckband with mattress stitch, unless otherwise stated.

Take care not to stretch the seams, especially around the back neck. It can be very easy to make the neck of a jacket or cardigan too wide, collars and edgings need to be stitched firmly into place, easing-in the back neck to fit the collar/edging rather then stretching the collar/edging to fit the back neck.

Straight cast-off sleeves: Place centre of cast-off edge of sleeve to shoulder seams. Sew top of sleeve to body, using markers as guidelines where applicable. Join side and sleeve seams.

Set-in sleeves: Join side and sleeve seams. Place centre of cast off edge of sleeve to shoulder seams. Set in sleeve, easing sleeve head into armhole.

CARE INSTRUCTIONS
Yarns

Follow the care instructions printed on each individual ball band. Where different yarns are used in the same garment, follow the care instructions for the more delicate one.

Buttons

We recommend that buttons are removed if your garment is to be machine washed.

ACKNOWLEDGEMENTS

Kathleen and I recognise that without the time and dedication of many brilliant people this book would not have been possible. As a mother and daughter team, special thanks goes to our loved ones, Malcolm, Richard and Lindsay for their constant support and encouragement throughout this project, and for their unfaltering belief in us.

We would like to express gratitude to our small but amazing team. Thank you all for making our vision a reality – Diana Fisher for the fabulous hair and make-up – Hannah Wright, our beautiful model, who makes this collection shine – Stella Smith and Sue Whiting, their pattern writing skills and keen eye are invaluable – Ella Taylor, Sandra Richardson and Arna Ronan whose knitting talents we value so highly, and Susan Laybourn for her time spent finishing the garments so superbly.

Our grateful thanks also go to Thelma Pickford for all her help at our fantastic location and David Cook for allowing us to take our photographs on his land. Finally Graham Watts for his fabulous photography and editorial creativity, and Angela Lin whose patience and professionalism was a joy throughout, to both, thank you for going above and beyond to ensure we have something pretty extraordinary.

INDEX